THE Introvert's Complete Career Guide

THE Introvert's Complete Career Guide

From Landing a Job to Surviving, Thriving, and Moving on Up

JANE FINKLE

CAREER PRESS

This edition first published in 2019 by Career Press, an imprint of
Red Wheel/Weiser, LLC
With offices at:
65 Parker Street, Suite 7
Newburyport, MA 01950
www.redwheelweiser.com
www.careerpress.com

ISBN: 978-1-63265-131-0
Library of Congress Cataloging-in-Publication Data

Names: Finkle, Jane, author.
Title: The introvert's complete career guide : from landing a job, to
surviving, thriving, and moving on up / by Jane Finkle.
Description: Newburyport, MA : Career Press, 2018. | Includes
bibliographical references.
Identifiers: LCCN 2018038604 | ISBN 9781632651310 (6 x 9 pbk. :
alk. paper)
Subjects: LCSH: Introverts--Vocational guidance. | Success in business.
Classification: LCC HF5382.693 .F56 2018 | DDC 650.14--dc23
LC record available at https://lccn.loc.gov/2018038604

Cover design by Kathryn Sky-Peck
Interior by Gina Schenck
Typeset in Adobe Garamond Pro and Book Antiqua

Printed in Canada
MAR
10 9 8 7 6 5 4 3 2 1

To my parents, who were creative thinkers and encouraged me to pursue my interests.

And to the quiet ones who find the ingenuity and courage to find their voice and express it with power, however subtle.

CONTENTS

INTRODUCTION:

PEOPLE LIKE US

I am an introvert. This reality revealed itself when I was very young. My mother would hand me a pot and a few utensils, and sit me on the tiled kitchen floor where I'd play on my own for hours. My older brother, on the other hand, was not tuned inward. Speaking freely to any stranger in his path, he demanded my mother's attention with his nonstop chatter. So when I came on the scene, my mother was amazed by the difference in our personalities. It pleased her that I could entertain myself with the simplest of props and required minimal human interaction. Of course, I was not the first of our family's introverts—in fact, I come from a long line of them. My grandmother's entrepreneurial spirit was supported by my quiet immigrant grandfather, who was content staying behind the scenes. And my socially timid father chronically complained of upcoming social gatherings, though in the end he thoroughly enjoyed such events despite his reticent nature.

Throughout my early years, as the floor tiles yellowed and life unfolded, I remained soothed by tranquil activities. Arts and crafts and reading provided a welcome balance to the drama of school interactions and social events. However, my quiet and reserved manner didn't prevent me from cultivating friendships. In fact, my reluctance to trumpet myself as bright and bold proved instrumental in attracting many friends. Like reading a good book, I enjoyed listening to their stories and coming up with ways to solve their problems. Most of all, I took pleasure in helping them rewrite a chapter in their lives that would lead to a happy ending. Looking back, it is no surprise that my particular form of introversion led to a career in counseling.

Extroversion Versus Introversion

The nature of extroversion versus introversion sparks lively conversations regarding who demonstrates which of these tendencies and why. You may have already taken one of the online tests or the formal Myers Briggs (MBTI) inventory to discover where you fall on the spectrum. The MBTI assessment is a psychometric questionnaire that attempts to measure psychological preferences for how people perceive the world and make decisions. Conceptualized and developed by Katherine Briggs and her daughter, Isabel Myers, the MBTI is based on psychiatrist Carl Jung's personality theory of psychological type. According to CPP Inc., the publisher of the MBTI instrument, it's "the world's most widely used personality assessment."[1]

It is natural to want to fit into a category that gives us an identity, especially if that identity provides a better understanding of ourselves and others, and explains the nature of our interactions. But be careful of typecasting yourself. Instead, try to think of extroversion and introversion as natural preferences, rather than hard and fast, glued-on labels.

The Theory

Where did all the hype about introversion and extroversion start? Carl Jung developed the theory known as "psychological type," which characterizes people into personality patterns. According to Jung, extroversion and introversion represent two of these personality patterns that focus on a person's expression of energy.[2] Extroverts are more energized when they have access to a wide and colorful palette of opportunities in the external world. Their energy expands and blooms when they are in the company of other people and engaged in a flurry of activity. An introvert's energy, on the other hand, draws deeply from their internal world. Less showy and overt, they enjoy a life of solitude, so they can explore their feelings and ideas from within and reflect undisturbed on life.

The Myth of Introversion

An introvert is often portrayed as someone who lacks social skills, a person who prefers to peek out from behind the curtain, satisfied to remain a spectator. In contrast, extroverts are viewed as social butterflies who bask assuredly in the limelight, assuming their place is at center stage. Although the social swirl of life in which we engage can reflect our personality type, this common perception is not entirely accurate. The difference between introversion and extroversion has, in fact, much more to do with how we express and channel our energy.

Contrary to popular belief, introverts are not necessarily shy or anti-social. Instead, they are often sharp observers and listen well. Generally disinclined to barge in at the beginning of a meeting or social gathering, an introvert will likely stay quiet and reflective as the more effusive extroverts jump in to offer comments. Good listeners by design, introverts prefer to take in all pertinent information before speaking, but then very often surprise their audience by making relevant, thoughtful contributions.

Are You an Introvert?

Answer the following questions to help determine whether or not your personality type falls within the spectrum of introversion:

a. I love chatting people up.
b. I hate small talk and like to get to the point.

a. I am more interested in what's happening around me.
b. I am more interested in my own thoughts and feelings.

a. I am often described as energetic and active.
b. I am often described as calm and reserved.

a. I enjoy working with groups more than working independently on my own.
b. I can work with groups but crave time to work alone.

a. I am one of the first to respond to a sudden or unexpected question.
b. I hope that someone else responds first to a sudden or unexpected question.

a. I tell it like it is.
b. I keep my thoughts close to the vest.

a. I tend to think out loud.
b. I think before I speak.

a. I easily initiate conversations at networking and social events.
b. I enjoy listening to people when I first meet them at networking and social events.

a. I enjoy going out with friends or family on a weekend night.
b. I enjoy staying at home with a good book or movie on a weekend night.

a. I have a general idea of what I will talk about at a meeting.
b. I plan in advance specifically what I am going to say at a meeting.

a. I can stay to the bitter end at a good party.
b. I am ready to leave the party after a few hours.

If you answered b more frequently than a, it is likely that you lean toward introversion. However, if you still feel unsure of where you fall on the scale of extroversion and introversion, check off the following words that describe you best, and see where your instinctive tendencies place you.

Introversion	Extroversion
Give people energy	Draw energy from people
Reflective	Active
Reserved	Outgoing
Quiet	Expressive
Daydreamer	Reality
Observer	Highly active
Private	Open
Solitude	Attracted to groups
Depth	Breadth
Don't enjoy small talk	Talkative
Serious	Easygoing
Think before speaking	Think and talk at the same time
Deep concentration	Easily distracted

If you selected eight or more words from the introversion list, you likely lean toward an introverted personality type.

Are You an Intro-Extrovert?

If you came out in the middle when you completed the questionnaire or found yourself identifying with both sides of the word chart, you might be what I like to call an "intro-extrovert." As I mentioned earlier, these personality types are merely preferences—not set in stone—and can therefore be influenced. The environment, for example, can enhance or otherwise affect personality type. Even if you consider yourself naturally introverted, you might experience situations that require more extroverted skills. As you develop these skills, you might achieve a higher comfort level, moving the needle of personality type a bit further to the extroversion side of the scale.

When I worked at the University of Pennsylvania, it was crucial to reach out to students, faculty, and staff to develop programs across different divisions. Equally important was to build relationships with key stakeholders. Even though I considered myself firmly placed on the introvert side of the scale, I was forced to employ more extroverted skills. Though at first this felt neither natural nor comfortable, the need to exercise new muscles built my confidence and proved to be a satisfying surprise. As time went on, I found that I began to actually enjoy stepping out in person and online to build my personal and professional network. However, even today my personality combines the two types; as good as I felt about discovering pleasure in situations challenging to introverts, I admit that I often dread large networking events.

Cultural Differences

To determine where you fall on the introvert scale, consider that introversion may also be characteristic of your culture. A recent study by psychologist Robert McCrae revealed that out of thirty-six cultures, Asian cultures and some African cultures identified more closely with introversion.[3] This is likely a result of both cultures' emphasis on tradition, conservatism, and compliance. This prevalence of introversion has by no means impeded the success of these cultures. On the contrary, a recent nationwide survey conducted by PEW Research Center revealed that Asian Americans are the best educated, earn the highest incomes, and constitute the fastest growing racial group in the United States.[4]

In America, we live in a culture that favors extroversion. Initiative is rewarded, speaking out is cheered, and taking action is applauded. For an introvert, unfortunately, this reality can leave one walking in an extrovert's shadow. To lead happy, productive, and successful lives in this culture, introverts must first understand and appreciate their personal value, and then balance the introversion with a sprinkling of extrovert skills.

In working with introverted clients, I often found that regardless of their circumstances—whether meeting with great success in their workplace or on the job hunt, seeking a new start—many questioned their personal value and ability to compete in the face of market changes. Taking cues from their experiences as well as my own personal challenges, I felt compelled to explore and uncover ways introverts can build on their strengths and confidently compete for new opportunities. These discoveries helped me create tools to help my clients at all life stages and professional levels succeed in their careers; this, in turn, inspired me to write a book that would pass this knowledge on to other introverts, endowing them with self-acceptance, and enabling them to shine.

Today's Whirlwind of Work

As a naturally careful and astute observer, you might have noticed the momentum of change in the workplace in recent years. Latching onto a job you think will whisk you along within the company as you make a steady climb up the corporate ladder until retirement is a thing of the past. With all the mobile gadgets at our disposal, we spend hours at work and beyond responding to chats, posts, texts, and emails. *New York Times* columnist Tom Friedman refers to this current phenomenon as the "age of acceleration."[5] In our attempt to keep up with the fast pace of technological advances and withstand the undeniable impact of globalization, we find ourselves in a breathless race.

These trends are producing a new kind of uncertainty in the workplace. Artificial intelligence and automation have displaced workers in many traditional jobs. And although new jobs are still being created, many employers are finding ways to streamline costs by hiring independent contractors or temporary workers as opposed to filling permanent positions. This reality has set in motion the gig economy (hiring for a single project or task), adding to the unpredictability of the job market. There are no firm statistics on the current percentage of US gig workers compared to permanent ones, but research conducted in 2015 by labor economists Lawrence F. Katz of Harvard and Alan B. Krueger of Princeton found that gig workers already made up 15.8 percent of the US workforce.[6] It's predicted that the number of gig workers will rise significantly by 2020.

One of the most essential survival tools in this age of acceleration is entrepreneurial skill. Although you don't actually have to become an entrepreneur yourself, your task is to think like one. Consider this new approach to your career as the "start-up of you," a phrase coined (and discussed in their bestselling book of the same title) by LinkedIn founder Reid Hamilton and entrepreneur Ben Casnocha.[7] From this view, your professional success depends on keeping yourself directed and creating your own professional opportunities. As an investor in your personal start-up, you will achieve a competitive edge by building problem-solving skills, exercising creative thinking, sharpening written and verbal communications talents, and furthering relationship-building and collaboration. In the current workplace, the never-ending flux and controlled chaos flowing from technological acceleration will also call upon personal qualities such as initiative, curiosity, flexibility, adaptability, and resiliency.

To keep that competitive edge sharp and bright in the fray of the work world, you will need to take a deep breath, accept risk, commit to lifelong learning, and tap into professional networks. So how does this environment affect introverts in particular? How do they overcome their natural anxieties to compete with extroverts and get the credit or promotions they deserve? Introverts in the workplace confront two major challenges they find especially difficult, but there are solutions.

Problems Introverts Face
and How to Solve Them

Competitive, rapidly changing, and unstable (especially in the gig economy and age of acceleration) are the norms in today's workplace. It's an environment in which extroverts thrive but introverts often struggle. Two areas in particular cause introverts to stumble:

Demonstrate Value to Employers

Employees must perform at the highest level by solving problems, delivering positive outcomes, and introducing and/or implementing innovations and new ideas. Most important, they must shine a light on their accomplishments, as well as on their talents and skills that generated them.

This can be particularly difficult for introverts because achieving success in this environment will require speaking up, promoting oneself and one's ideas, and taking initiative beyond the basic responsibilities of the job—all areas they can find challenging. As a result, they tend to stand on the sidelines while social dynamos with the skills and confidence to take initiative and toot their own horns get the jobs, the promotions, and all the attention.

This book will teach you techniques that help introverts use reflective skills to formulate their thoughts and ideas so they can express themselves clearly and confidently in a network meeting, interview, or a variety of workplace situations. You will also find tools such as a personal characteristics exercise that generates a list of top ten personal adjectives—versatile terms that make it easy to add color and depth to a resume, or to respond to the common interview question, "Can you tell me about yourself?" Last, I provide sample scripts for presenting oneself in a powerful thirty-second introduction that will alleviate the introvert's anxiety about meeting people they don't know.

Cultivate and Maintain Relationships

Relationships in the workplace offer mentoring and support on important projects, knowledge on current trends in that field or industry, and reinforce chances for future career opportunities. Introverts are fully capable of sustaining good relationships, but because they tend to favor privacy (that is, they are loners), they often don't recognize the essential role relationships play in their ability to succeed in a job or career. Nor do they understand how best to reach out to initiate such relationships.

To support relationship-building, this book offers seven steps for cultivating and communicating effectively with a new employer or client. It also includes eight keys to career survival and moving ahead in one's career, outlining steps you can take to ensure you get noticed, either in your office or in a virtual context. These are just some of the tools that will help you confidently build rapport and effectively communicate with senior leaders and colleagues.

My Story

As an introvert, I approach this topic with understanding, compassion, and some hard-earned wisdom. I was a career counselor at the University of Pennsylvania working with undergraduate liberal arts and business students, as well as alumni. My track record of helping students identify career goals and help them find employment was very good, but because I was too shy to speak up at staff meetings, I couldn't get attention for my new ideas and programs, let alone my past accomplishments. As a result, my colleagues and supervisors were not aware of my previous achievements or current projects, and I missed out on valuable opportunities and promotions.

Fortunately, my new boss observed my capabilities and encouraged me to take more credit for my counseling successes and innovative program ideas. She selected me to serve on various university committees and present reports to senior level staff. In time, I won my battle with fear by taking risks that led to building confidence. When I finally spoke up and took credit for the good work I was doing, I was then promoted to the position of associate director for Wharton undergrads, directing career services and supervising staff and graduate interns.

I knew I had to conquer my fear of self-promotion if I wanted to move toward my ultimate goal of becoming an entrepreneur with my own consulting business in career counseling. I simply had to overcome the "invisible woman" syndrome I had brought on by my own introverted tendencies!

Once again, I accomplished this by acknowledging my fears and gradually taking action. I reached out to my many professional contacts for advice and started to develop my expertise as a public speaker, presenting workshops at a variety of organizations. I designed and wrote content for my website, forced myself to grow my professional network substantially through LinkedIn, and took on leadership roles in professional associations. I also wrote and posted career advice articles on my blog and on social media.

Although I tried to conquer the introverted tendencies holding me back, I noticed that some of these characteristics could actually be used to my advantage. For instance, I discovered that my quiet manner of listening carefully to a client's story allowed me to observe her or his problems in a deep and focused way; this translated to a real listening skill. Then, because I needed time to arrange my thoughts until I felt ready to speak up and offer advice, I found that I possessed a deeper understanding of the roadblocks he or she faced than if I had spoken up immediately. This contemplative approach transferred to a strong analytic ability on my part and, in turn, led to becoming an effective problem-solver who is capable of devising good solutions for my clients.

Eventually, I developed a series of successful tools specifically designed to help introverts overcome blocks to strong performance. To accomplish this, I combined insights from my observations on my clients' problems and behaviors with those from my deep study of the psychological literature, especially *Happenstance Learning Theory* by John Krumboltz, *Learned Optimism* by Martin Seligman, and Aaron Beck's cognitive behavioral theory. I also utilized my formal training as a Myers Briggs assessment specialist. (I evaluated results of the inventory given to those who wished to find out more about their personality and its impact on career choice and work environment.)

My system proves to be successful because it focuses on the areas in which introverts struggle most: self-promotion, taking the risk of revealing oneself in person and online, taking initiative, speaking up at meetings and networking events, reaching out to colleagues to form good relationships, and being forceful in meetings. After my clients use the tools and techniques, they report that they feel less fearful and more confident about expressing who they are and what they have to offer when networking, using social media, and in interviews. Meanwhile, those already employed say they now understand what steps to take to advance in their existing job. This system constitutes the heart of *The Introvert's Complete Career Guide*.

1

GIVE THE WALLFLOWER A VOICE

Introverts tend to possess the ability for intense concentration and a sense of calm and compassion, as well as being perceptive, observant, and good listeners, according to the Myers Briggs personality type definitions and studies by psychologist Marti Olsen Laney, PsyD, MFT, author of *The Introvert Advantage: How to Thrive in an Extrovert World*.[1]

However, when you think about your own introverted personality, you're likely to focus on the negative aspects of your reserved nature, such as not speaking up or taking action. Like a wallflower, you may feel invisible and ignored as the laughter and fun of the party swirl around you.

Being quiet and thoughtful can have a calming effect on your friends and colleagues, but those personality traits won't propel your job search or win you that promotion. However, if you take advantage of your ability to concentrate and think problems through, you can become as successful as any extrovert. After all, even wallflowers can blossom! It all begins with focusing on your positive personal attributes and having a clear and deep understanding of what you bring to the table.

I found that one of the big challenges for many introverts is expressing what makes them unique, especially in situations when there's no time to think through possible answers. Questions such as, "How would you describe yourself?" or "What are your strengths?" are examples of what you'll be asked when exploring a new career, looking for a job, talking to an acquaintance who may have a lead, or sitting in an interview. As introverts, we share information about ourselves as if we are peeling away the layers of an onion, gradually opening up as we get to know someone better. However, employers and professional contacts may expect answers they can sink their teeth into immediately—a full-fledged "meal" of information, complete with details and insights into what makes you tick and how you might add value to the industry or field.

Self-Assessment: Who Are You, Really?

If you want to succeed in your career now and in the future, it's essential to understand how to clearly articulate who you are and the scope of your experience. Most introverts know deep down what makes them special, but finding the right words to express their uniqueness can prove to be challenging. Even when you embrace the words, it's not your nature to boast, so understanding how to come across as talented and competent without sounding egotistical can be equally tricky.

Going through a self-assessment process is like unwrapping a gift of self-awareness that offers you both insight into your strengths and the language to sell yourself to the professional world. I designed the series of exercises in this chapter to help you identify and evaluate your achievements, values, skills, interests, and personality, providing a keen awareness of what you bring to the table and the confidence to express these attributes to a contact or prospective employer.

Maybe you don't trust that completing a series of exercises will help you overcome your panic about what to say when a prospective employer or networking contact asks those big questions. Stay tuned, because I am about to show how a full inventory of *you* will offset your fear or self-doubt. The self-assessment process takes advantage of your natural, introverted penchant for "digging deep" or seeking within. You'll uncover unique strengths and capabilities, and discover what's important to you. These insights can be used to create an engaging story that you'll be eager to tell about yourself at a networking event, in an informational meeting, on a LinkedIn profile, or during an interview or performance evaluation.

Achievements Exercise

Throughout your life, you can no doubt list a variety of achievements of which you deserve to be proud. They might be personal accomplishments like learning to fix a flat tire, running a 5K, cooking a gourmet meal, and organizing a family event; or career-related successes like writing a proposal, training staff, introducing a new program, or creating a database. Whether simple or complex, achievements can instill a sense of pride and boost confidence. They also offer clues into your overall interests, skills, and values, and will generate words and phrases you can use to describe who you are and what your goals are. After you complete these exercises, you'll know exactly what to say about your achievements and how these reflect your added value to people who can support your job search or as you promote your career to potential employers.

Shining a bright light on your achievements is one of the most positive ways to understand what has been most meaningful to you in your life. Completing the following achievement exercise is also a great way to get out of your introverted modesty zone and give your ego an overdue massage as you take pride in your many accomplishments.

When I taught a career evaluation course at the University of Pennsylvania, I used myself to model the Achievement Exercise by listing three of my favorite achievements, and then asking my students for feedback on what they learned about me based upon these accomplishments.

My Three Accomplishments

1. Creating my first flower garden.
2. Getting selected by my high school English department to recite the Gettysburg Address before a large audience at the end of the town Memorial Parade. I managed to do it in spite of my fear of being in the spotlight.

3. Designing, planning, and presenting the first career discovery seminar for college students at the University of Pennsylvania's Wharton School of Business.

I asked the class to help me identify any interests and skills related to my three accomplishments as well as corresponding values (standards or ideals important to a person, such as using one's creativity or obtaining recognition—the two values demonstrated in the following Gettysburg Address example). What they came up with for each of my achievements expanded on what I knew about myself!

My Three Accomplishments' Skills and Values

1. **Planting my first flower garden**
    ⇨ **Skills:** visual design, creative thinking, planning, problem-solving
    ⇨ **Values:** aesthetics, creativity, learning

2. **Gettysburg Address**
    ⇨ **Skills:** public speaking, performing
    ⇨ **Values:** recognition, creativity

3. **Career Discovery Seminar**
    ⇨ **Skills:** research, writing, interviewing, teaching, advising, organizing, problem-solving, creative thinking
    ⇨ **Values:** creativity, knowledge, recognition, helping others

My Essential Skills and Values

From this point, I asked my students to boil down all this information to the essence of my key skills and values. The result was as follows:

⇨ **Skills:** written and verbal communications, problem-solving, public speaking, and counseling/advising

⇨ **Values:** creativity, recognition, and knowledge

I have used their analysis many times to respond to the request "Describe yourself" and to answer the question "What are your strengths?" Keep in mind that you don't have to be an Olympic champion to feel accomplished. Achievements can be career related, personal, or a combination of both. These can be challenges that you've met, successes you've achieved in creating projects or initiatives, or even a simple act of kindness.

Identify at least three achievements that make you proud, plus the skills and values attached to each and write them down in this order:

⇨ Achievement

⇨ Skills

⇨ Values

Think all the way back to high school. Maybe you were on the track team, wrote for the school paper, or served as class or club officer. In college, writing an outstanding research paper, studying abroad, and volunteering for Habitat for Humanity are all examples of major achievements. At work, consider your successes with challenging projects or tasks, reports, presentations, leadership roles, and innovations.

You may also want to ask colleagues or friends to review your list and see if they can add others. If you're an introvert, you might well have overlooked some gems.

Values: What's My Purpose?

To gain the most insight into what you find meaningful, let's consider what "values" mean and why this is significant. On its own, the term can imply one's principles or criteria, but here it reflects the many potential facets of how you envision your ideal work—your physical environment, the type of work you are doing, or the philosophy behind it.

Why Values Offer Important Clues to Your Happiness

As you look for new job opportunities or promotions, you want to make sure the jobs you're pursuing support your most important values. If you feel something is missing in your work, it is a sign that some of your values are being compromised. On the other hand, when your work is clearly rewarding, it means that your daily tasks and work environment are aligned with your career values. For example, if you value creativity, you might enjoy working in advertising or graphic design.

To pinpoint your personal values, ask yourself the following career value–oriented questions.

1. Is working with other people more appealing than working alone?

2. Do you like your responsibilities to be clearly structured, or do you prefer some room for creativity?

3. Do you want to work in an environment that helps people? Or one in which you make systems or procedures more effective?

Understanding which values are most important to you from the outset will provide a compass for carefully navigating your career choices and decisions in your work life. It will also provide direction on how to articulate your motivations and goals. When it comes to values, an introvert's natural tendency to look inward will work in your favor since you're always on a quest for meaning.

Values Exercise

Review the following list, and select five values that you feel best support your career and life goals right now.

⇨ **Social concerns:** Do something that contributes to the common good.

⇨ **Help others:** Get directly involved with helping people individually or in small groups.

⇨ **Public contact:** Have a lot of day-to-day interaction with people.

⇨ **Supportive relationships:** Have rewarding relationships with colleagues.

⇨ **Professional accomplishment:** Achieve high performance and career advancement.

⇨ **Make decisions:** Have the power to decide on courses of action and policies.

⇨ **Solitude:** Work on projects on your own.

⇨ **Competition:** Engage in activities that clearly compare your abilities to others.

⇨ **Power:** Influence and impact people and/or systems.

⇨ **Fast pace:** Work in situations where there is a lot of activity and tasks must be completed quickly.

⇨ **Work-life balance:** Achieve a healthy balance between work and personal life.

⇨ **Excitement:** Experience a high or frequent level of excitement and risk in your work.

⇨ **Wealth:** Earn a substantial salary for your work.

⇨ **Recognition:** Receive public acknowledgement for the quality of your work.

⇨ **Independence:** Determine the nature of your work without significant direction from others.

⇨ **Integrity:** Feel that work contributes to a set of morals that are important to you.

⇨ **Location:** Find a place to live that is conducive to your lifestyle.

⇨ **Knowledge:** Engage in the pursuit of knowledge and truth.

⇨ **Intellectual status:** Become an expert in a given field.

⇨ **Creativity:** Generate new ideas for programs, written materials, and organization.

⇨ **Vision:** Get involved in future direction and big-picture thinking.

⇨ **Aesthetics:** Study or appreciate the beauty of objects and ideas.

⇨ **Change and variety:** Have work responsibilities that frequently change.

⇨ **Challenge:** Take on difficult or demanding tasks or advance your skills.

⇨ **Accuracy:** Work in settings where details are important and there is little margin for error.

⇨ **Security:** Feel confident about keeping your job and reaping a reasonable financial reward.

Now determine how many of your top values are satisfied in your current work situation. Also consider how you would like these values to support you in the future. For example, if "Power" and "Make decisions" are priorities, consider what you can do to incorporate these in your everyday life, like starting your own business or looking for new job opportunities that will advance your leadership skills and responsibilities. If you're not working right now, think about how these values can help with your job search. For instance, if some of your foremost values are "Creativity," "Aesthetics," and "Excitement," then fashion, entertainment, and advertising are examples of career environments that could satisfy these choices. If your combination of essential values includes "Help others," "Social concerns," and "Professional advancement," you should express clearly in an interview with a professional contact or employer why choosing to work in a mission-driven organization is so important to you. Assessing and identifying what you find meaningful will allow you to articulate to a potential employer how you can add value to their company or organization.

In short, you should highlight your values in every stage of your job search strategy and career development, from writing a resume and preparing a social media profile to engaging in an interview and seeking a job promotion. Your values remain important themes throughout the entire story of your career.

The Seasoned Wallflower: Tom's Story

Tom is an introverted mid-career senior IT project manager who was laid off by a large corporation. Tom hadn't looked for a new job in fifteen years and wasn't sure if he wanted to return to a corporate environment that required being on call and working overtime. As we talked, I could see that Tom was sinking deeper into his chair. Like many talented introverts, he wasn't sure how to market his skills or experience, or how to speak in the kind of language that translates well to an employer via a resume, networking meeting, or interview.

After completing the values exercise, Tom saw that his top values were "Work-life balance," "Security," "Supportive relationships," "Creativity," and "Social concerns." This helped him consider new options such as foundations, government, and universities, all of which had the potential to support his values. More important, understanding his own values contributed to Tom's ability to answer interview questions about what made him a strong candidate besides his experience and technical skills.

Tom was able to respond to the question "What makes you a competitive candidate?" by telling the story of his career in a way that highlighted his values.

I have a strong record of assessing organizational IT problems and generating creative solutions ("Creativity") combined with a talent for cultivating relationships with colleagues, executive staff, and customers ("Supportive relationships"). I have been involved in community theater and enjoy an environment that is focused on providing cultural programs to the public. I would now like to contribute my experience and skills in a mission-driven organization ("Social concerns").

Using the profile, Tom found a new and exciting opportunity working in IT at a large foundation.

The process of evaluating your values and understanding what's meaningful to you will lead to the right words and phrases to use in all phases of your job search and working toward promotions. Armed with this information, you will find that your fear of not knowing what to say or how to say it will fade away.

THE WALLFLOWER IN FULL BLOOM

In today's marketplace, the competition for securing a good job is steep, and demonstrating high performance is a must for advancing one's career. Introverts can rely on strengths such as creating calm and using a thoughtful perspective to enhance their position in the workplace, but it is equally important that they express what makes them unique and competent. This can be challenging to introverts if they are asked to say more about who they are or to go into detail about their strengths. This chapter takes the self-assessment process a few steps further by providing exercises to help articulate in greater detail who you are and what skills you bring to your industry or profession.

What Color Is My Personality?

Personality plays a strong role in how an employer or professional contact views your ability to work with managers, colleagues, customers, and clients. As an introvert, you might freeze up when faced with questions that feel personal because you don't like to reveal too much about yourself to a stranger or you might come across as a braggart. However, if you defer too much to the cautious and shy side of your personality, you won't come through in full color.

Ask yourself if you can answer this question quickly with four to five adjectives or phrases: "If I had a group of your colleagues here and asked them to describe you, what would they say?" Don't fret if you found this challenging. You're going to complete a simple personality characteristics exercise, and once you finish it, you'll end up with several adjectives for your job search toolbox.

Personal Characteristics Exercise

Pick ten to twelve words from the following list on pages 24 and 25 that you think best describe your personality. Similar to the choices you made in the values exercise, this exercise summarizes and articulates what you believe to be your strongest personality traits via an interview, resume, or LinkedIn profile. Essentially, this method forces you to think about which combination of characteristics paints the most accurate picture of you that is also the most compelling to employers. In addition to the terms listed here, feel free to add any others that you consider most fitting.

Adaptable	Leader	Practical	Sensitive
Ambitious	Assertive	Introspective	Analytical
Diplomatic	Friendly	Enthusiastic	Adventurous
Decisive	Fearful	Organized	Idealistic
Brave	Calm	Cautious	Complex
Creative	Humorous	Conscientious	Open-minded
Serious	Listener	Spontaneous	Stubborn
Curious	Rigid	Articulate	Goal oriented
Independent	Passive	Honest	Loyal
Optimistic	Reserved	Anxious	Pessimistic

Quiet	Argumentative	Imaginative	Competitive
Conforming	Compassionate	Perfectionistic	Persuasive
Perceptive	Inconsistent	Respectful	Self-disciplined
Self-assured	Strong	Intelligent	Judgmental
Cooperative	Determined	Critical	Supportive
Questioning	Consistent	Flexible	Defensive
Professional	Responsible	Shy	Risk averse
Fun-loving	Stable	Poised	Quick learner
Reliable	Authentic	Caring	Self-conscious

You might want to take this exercise one step further and ask three people, such as a friend, a colleague, and a relative, to select ten to twelve adjectives that *they* think best describe you. Their lists will give you insight into how other people perceive you in comparison to how you see yourself. You may discover that others observe strengths you don't realize you have. Now when an employer asks you to describe your personality, you'll have at least ten words at your fingertips.

Some of the terms you selected may have a negative connotation (such as "inconsistent"). You obviously don't want to share this with a network-ing contact or employer, but it's still valuable to be aware of areas that need improvement. For our purposes, we will be focusing on adjectives that describe you in a positive way.

Let's take look at Joan, a successful but introverted woman who was flustered at the challenge of going back to work after a long hiatus.

The Reentering Wallflower: Joan's Story

Joan owned and managed a successful retail business for fifteen years, how-ever, she sold it when her elderly parents started to have health issues. She monitored their medical and living situation while balancing quality time with her husband and children. During her ten-year gap from the traditional workplace, Joan became a dedicated volunteer, raising money for a community association and serving on the board of a nonprofit organization. After receiving an award for her bold fundraising efforts, Joan decided to pursue opportunities in fundraising and development and came to me for help.

Joan had not written a resume in ten years and was nervous about what to include. As we began, she downplayed her experience and personal attributes (as introverts tend to do). Though successful in fundraising, she had trouble asserting herself to a potential employer. So I had her complete the personal characteristics exercise to build her confidence and generate words to describe herself in the job search process. When it came time to draft a profile, or "summary" (see Chapter 3 for a full discussion on resume writing), we selected terms from her results like "Ambitious," "Decisive," "Creative," and "Intelligent." We also plugged some of these key terms into her LinkedIn profile (see Chapter 4 for more on social media profiles), as this is now a common practice to incorporate a few personal characteristics. Here is what we came up with for Joan's profile:

> *Dynamic business professional with substantial experience in management and fundraising. Expertise in event planning, researching and soliciting donors, proposal writing, and project management. Talent for cultivating and maintaining strong relationships with colleagues and donors. Ambitious, creative, and decisive.*

Because she completed the personal characteristics exercise, Joan felt she was able to better articulate who she was not only in cover letters and resumes, but also in person. Consequently, she obtained a great opportunity in fundraising at an arboretum. In this position she plans and organizes events, as well as researches and develops strategies for attracting prospective donors.

Skills: Put Your Competence on Display

Employers want to learn more about your areas of expertise in their field or industry, but they are equally interested in finding out which skills you bring to the job, from how you communicate with others to your knowledge of social media and your ability to manage projects. For most introverts, extracting skills from your experience is the easiest part of this self-assessment process because it doesn't feel particularly personal. But don't minimize the importance of digging deeper and exploring further into your experience to offer a wider picture of your talents and skills.

Start by reviewing a description of your current job responsibilities or a recently posted job opportunity and then make a list of your related skills. Here are two examples of tasks and the skills they require.

⇨ **Task:** Creating and Delivering a Presentation
　　⇨ **Skills:** Researching, Writing and Editing Content, Organizing, Technical (PowerPoint), Visual Design, and Public Speaking

⇨ **Task:** Overseeing Company Budget
　　⇨ **Skills:** Quantitative, Analytical Thinking, Problem-Solving, Collaborating, Writing Reports, Projecting Revenues and Expenses, Enforcing Policies and Procedures

To feel fully confident about what you have to offer, complete this exercise, as well as the following inventory, to generate a comprehensive list of your skills.

Skills Inventory

Select from this list any skills that you believe reflect your strengths, and add any additional ones specifically related to your field or industry.

Communication

⇨ Proficient or fluent in other languages

⇨ Write or edit articles, blogs, or social media content

⇨ Persuade or influence others

⇨ Create effective presentations

⇨ Collaborate with teams and groups

⇨ Cultivate and build relationships

⇨ Public speaking

⇨ Write proposals and reports

⇨ Debate

⇨ Listen

⇨ Negotiate

⇨ Marketing/Selling/Promoting

Creative

⇨ Create websites

⇨ Graphic design

⇨ Production/AV skills

⇨ Brainstorm new ideas and strategies/Inventive

⇨ Build from scratch

⇨ Creative writing

⇨ Visual arts

⇨ Compose music

⇨ Perform in theater, dance, or film

Financial

⇨ Manage and monitor budget

⇨ Oversee organization's finances

⇨ Project expenses and revenue

⇨ Calculate or reconcile expenses and revenue

⇨ Compare or evaluate costs

⇨ Succeed in work with strong quantitative focus

Support

⇨ Teach/Train

⇨ Counsel/Advise/Support

⇨ Mediate/Conflict resolution

⇨ Advocate for individuals, special populations, causes

⇨ Facilitate group discussions and meetings

Organization/Management

⇨ Generate solutions for organizational issues

⇨ Understand and enforce policies and procedures

⇨ Navigate complex bureaucratic environments

⇨ Plan, organize, and implement events and programs

⇨ Use timelines, checklists, flowcharts, outlines, or other organizational tools

⇨ Work effectively under pressure and meet deadlines

⇨ Build organizational systems and procedures

Leadership

⇨ Oversee small and/or large groups comfortably

⇨ Delegate work

⇨ Listen to ideas and help reach consensus

⇨ Evaluate team members' performance and provide professional development

⇨ Manage projects from beginning to end

⇨ Identify goals and/or tasks to be accomplished and completed

⇨ Motivate groups or individuals to meet goals

Technical

⇨ Assemble components

⇨ Handle instruments

⇨ Knowledge of software systems and computer languages

⇨ Manage and input data

⇨ Learn and adapt to new technologies

⇨ Understand how to operate equipment

⇨ Construct or build physical materials

Research/Analysis

⇨ Identify problems, research goals, and reach conclusions

⇨ Understand, evaluate, and synthesize data

⇨ Design and analyze surveys

⇨ Locate and assimilate new information quickly

Now that you completed the self-assessment exercises, where do you go from here? James, a typical, quiet introvert with a successful career in law and finance, shows us one path forward.

The Mid-Career Wallflower: James's Story

James is a soft-spoken, intense Ivy League graduate who earned both an MBA and law degree. After completing his graduate studies, he accepted an associate's position at a large law firm. However, James predicted that his career would not advance unless he could generate new clients by joining in the firm's social events. He wasn't incapable of meeting these expectations; rather, as an introvert, he simply disliked the pressure to socialize and network for clients.

After five years at the firm, James left for an an economics and law position at a financial service firm working in compliance and regulatory affairs. He enjoyed the tasks as well as the occasion to work alone for a portion of the day even though he was part of a larger team. The laser-sharp focus required for success in this job appealed to him, too.

Even though the position was well suited to James, he wasn't advancing to higher levels of management, so he asked me to help him find a new job. When I first met with him, James was able to articulate his major responsibilities and what he liked about his work, but offered little information about results or positive outcomes of his efforts. When I asked him if his supervisor and senior executive team were aware of his accomplishments and success in meeting performance goals, he said he believed his colleagues and managers should know he was a strong performer simply by observing him in the workplace. It was clear that if James learned to be more vocal in promoting his achievements and skills to his supervisors, he wouldn't need to look elsewhere for a job; he could just land a promotion. James needed to learn how to market himself.

After James completed the self-assessment exercises, I worked with him to come up with some strategies for moving beyond the "quiet and diligent worker" (as he described himself), and demonstrate directly and strongly the value of his work to his employer. These strategies focused on the following areas.

Enhance Visibility

Some of the key skills on James's self-assessment included "Analytical thinking," "Problem-solving," and "Writing reports." He used these skills to complete an in-depth analysis of how to reduce risks and client costs that would favorably impact his division. I suggested that he make an effort to showcase this analysis to upper management since it represented a significant achievement. Based on our discussion, James put together a PowerPoint presentation of his findings from the analysis and asked to present this report to the senior executive team. Because he had time to carefully develop and think through the report, James's presentation was successful as his supervisor and senior executives witnessed his skills in use and, ultimately, his value to the department.

Demonstrate High Performance

In the past, James took a passive role regarding his annual evaluation, hoping that his performance would speak for itself and would earn him positive results. This time, just before his upcoming evaluation, I had James pull out a few more work accomplishments from his self-assessment to plan in advance what he wanted to say about his performance during his review. One of his more impressive accomplishments was taking on a leadership role for a team compliance project. This required James to use a variety of skills to mediate conflicts among team members, organize timelines, delegate tasks, and motivate the team to generate productive results. Not only was the project a success, it also supported some of James's key values: "Challenge," "Knowledge," "Building relationships," and "Integrity."

James was confident and well prepared for his performance evaluation, and with several examples, he showed how his compliance project, risk analysis report, and other accomplishments contributed to both the division and the company overall. As a result of his presentation, James received a promotion within six months. His clear understanding of his accomplishments, values, and skills supported James in letting go of his familiar role as the competent but invisible professional. Most important, it also gave James the power he needed to speak up and demonstrate to his employers both the degree of his capability and the difference his work made to the company.

Additional Self-Assessment Information

You should also generate a list of your outside interests or volunteer activities. Some employers like to break the ice by asking what you enjoy doing outside of work. Or you may discover that you share similar interests, such as running marathons. During an interview I was once asked, "Who is one of your favorite authors?" As an avid reader, I was able to offer a quick reply: "Richard Russo" (who happens to be from my hometown). This led to an interesting exchange, as the interviewer was familiar with Russo, and then volunteered a few of her own favorite authors. This conversation about books helped build a good rapport, while the interviewer learned something about me and my tastes. Our common interest served to make a positive connection during the interview.

The following questions are designed to help you get in touch with your own personal interests, aspirations, and more.

⇨ What types of activities and hobbies do I enjoy?

⇨ What are my natural talents?

⇨ What did I like to do as a child or adolescent?

⇨ What principles, causes, or issues are important to me?

⇨ What are some of my favorite books, TV shows, and movies?

⇨ What characteristics do people compliment me on?

⇨ What would I do if I had all the money in the world?

⇨ What training or class would I like to take if I had more time?

⇨ What dreams have I postponed?

Self-Assessment Summary

To help keep all of this information organized, create a chart or a list that summarizes your self-assessment work in the following categories:

⇨ Achievements

⇨ Values

⇨ Skills

⇨ Personal characteristics

⇨ Interests

⇨ Outside activities

Hold on to the summary, as you'll pull information from your self-assessment as we progress through the book. The summary will take you all the way from the initial phases of the job search to establishing a strong presence in your current or new job.

When Tom, Joan, and James stepped back to carefully examine their accomplishments, strengths, personal qualities, and values, they discovered they each possessed a strong voice. Having completed the exercises in these first two chapters, you know more about how you relate to the world of work, and have a voice that speaks the language of competence and confidence.

TELL YOUR STORY

It's a given: Expertly crafted resumes that draw a rich self-portrait contribute to a successful job search, leading to new career opportunities. The resume provides a perfect canvas for introverts to shine and bring their unique qualifications and hard-earned skills into the spotlight. Working quietly behind the scenes, you can dig deep into your experience, unearth your achievements, and dust off your industry knowledge and personal qualities.

Introverts tend to feel somewhat uncomfortable blowing their own horn both in life and in a resume. Therefore, they might overlook accomplishments or tasks that deserve applause. But in the current competitive and innovative economy where results matter, you must prove to employers that you are a high performer or risk losing a great opportunity. So don't be afraid to trumpet your legacy of experiences and achievements in an eye-catching script on your resume. Your purpose is not to brag, but to reveal just how you can bring value to an organization. A resume that puts your best foot forward builds deserved self-confidence and reinforces your personal worth.

In this chapter, we will develop strategies that portray you as a results-oriented professional through your resume. You won't need to magically become an extrovert to make this happen.

Five Resume Trends

Count to six. This is how long many recruiters take to review your resume, according to a recent survey by Ladders, an online job-matching service.[1] The reality that all your hard work is boiled down to such a quick, off-hand perusal can be difficult to imagine. This approach to resume review can vary depending on the employer and company hiring procedures, but your resume has to stand out from the crowd. Whether it's six seconds or one minute, the resume must always shout, "Hey! I'm here, and you need me!" in the first glance. The speed of review has transformed the traditional resume into a document that is tighter, shorter, and leaner.

Considering the time employers allot to each candidate, how do you get their attention? Employers are looking for five basic trends, so incorporating these into your resume is the best way to catch their eye and convince them you are the optimal candidate. These five trends can be summarized as follows:

1. **Achievements:** While employers quickly review your position title along with your basic responsibilities and tasks, what they primarily look for is results. Achievements that demonstrate outcomes, innovation, and problem-solving can spell out how you add value and exemplify high performance.

2. **Personal branding:** What differentiates you from every other candidate? Personal branding gives employers a snapshot of who you are by highlighting your accomplishments, contributions, talent, passion, and vision. By incorporating branding into your resume, you show employers what makes you unique.

3. **Short-and-sweet descriptions:** Keep your descriptions brief and to the point. Think shorter paragraphs and tighter sentences.

4. **Keywords:** These are specific words and phrases that help employers quickly evaluate if you are the best fit among the multitude of other candidates. Therefore, the strategic use of such terms throughout your resume can be an important factor in getting through initial screenings. Today, many employers use computer sourcing and applicant tracking systems (ATS) that track candidates by keywords, so the frequency and choice of keywords is significant.

5. **Visual presentation:** Technology has made it possible to add some punch to your resume with color and design elements like charts. Subtle details like blue lines or gray headings can add energy to a black-and-white page. Alternatively, if you prefer a more traditional format, color is not required to create a winning look.

If you feel your introverted voice of apprehension coming through on any of these trends, don't fret. I will incorporate these into my discussion as I lead you through key points of writing a powerful resume.

Start With a Strategy

Take advantage of your ability to concentrate in order to reach your resume's starting line: focusing on your industry/field and target audience. What specific experiences, talents, achievements, and personal qualities lead to success in your field? Answers to these questions will help identify keywords and build a strong foundation for your resume. The following examples show professional areas paired with functions directly related to their industries, as well as personal qualities that often define success in those fields.

Sales

⇨ Related functions: Expanding territory, exceeding quota, networking

⇨ Personal qualities: Enthusiastic, gregarious, competitive

Senior Executive

⇨ Related functions: Business development, innovation, leadership

⇨ Personal qualities: Decisive, ambitious, powerful

Teacher

⇨ Related functions: Learning environment, cultural diversity, curriculum

⇨ Personal qualities: Compassionate, creative, accepting

Biomedical Engineer

⇨ Related functions: Data analysis, thermal systems, prototype

⇨ Personal qualities: Perseverance, analytical, inventive

Now make a list of terms that fit your personal career experience and your job target. You will be able to use these in your headline and summary as well as your job descriptions. If you are a recent graduate, draw from experiences such as internships, leadership activities, or classroom projects. Reentering the workforce? Draw from activities with value such as volunteering, serving on community boards, taking professional courses, or training.

Achievements

Your dynamic work deserves an equally dynamic resume. Showcasing action-packed results through your admirable achievements is a big trend and an essential component of today's powerful resume.

What have you done so far in your career that speaks to your talents and skills? How have your special projects or initiatives produced significant results? When asking yourself these questions, consider what answers will convince a prospective employer that you are an attractive recruit.

Review your self-assessment chart from Chapter 2 and pull out signature, singular work accomplishments. You may also want to supplement the list with additional work achievements that you may have left off your initial list.

Some examples of compelling accomplishments might be:

⇨ Initiating and implementing a project, process, or procedure

⇨ Introducing new ideas, strategies, and techniques

⇨ Generating a productive solution to a problem

⇨ Streamlining costs or reducing waste

⇨ Increasing profits or revenue

⇨ Expanding programs

⇨ Securing funding

⇨ Creating innovation

Your soul may struggle with tooting your own horn and giving expression to the full scope of your achievements. Overcoming this reserve, however, is crucial. Otherwise you will miss a golden opportunity to promote yourself, and an employer may fail to notice a great potential employee. Using your natural ability to focus, surmount your hesitancy, and let your achievements represent an important chapter in the story of your career. Believe that you matter and what you have achieved is significant.

Accomplishment Descriptions: Before and After

Sheila is a high-performing introvert who almost concealed one of the most notable stories of her accomplishment. Once she revealed the details, her description was entirely transformed.

Sheila works for a marketing firm at which she designs and delivers social media campaigns to a variety of clients. One of her proudest accomplishments was the success of a social media campaign that she designed and delivered to an online clothing company. Her efforts were so effective, and the campaign so successful, that the client decided to totally replace their traditional marketing strategies with social media. Best of all, the client retained Sheila for future social media campaigns. This talented woman nearly sidestepped an ideal opportunity to tell the story of her fine work and the outcome of increasing business for her firm.

⇨ **Before:** Implemented successful B2C social media program.

⇨ **After:** Designed and implemented successful B2C social media program, resulting in client dropping traditional advertising campaigns and expanding engagement with marketing firm.

An achievement doesn't always have to be quantified, but leaving out desirable and tangible results may prove to be a fatal flaw. Without clear evidence, a prospective employer may have missed Sheila's unique ability to think creatively and build strong relationships that generate more business.

Scope-Contribution-Outcome (SCO)

SCO is a formula I developed to help my clients write standout achievement statements through a simple step-by-step process. It breaks down as follows:

⇨ **Scope:** Overview and breadth of project, task, or initiative

⇨ **Contribution:** Your actions

⇨ **Outcome:** The results that you achieved

The two following examples demonstrate how applying this formula can bring out a deeper level of facts and particulars to a person's accomplishments.

Director of Development

⇨ **Achievement:** Directed organization's membership program.

⇨ **Scope:** 500 full museum memberships and 900 complimentary memberships.

⇨ **Contribution:** Managed program, improved member benefits, increased membership programs.

⇨ **Outcome:** Increased membership and program's revenue from $22,000 to $40,000 in two years.

⇨ **Final achievement statement:** Directed organization's membership program serving 500 full museum members and 900 complimentary members. Expanded and improved benefits and programs increasing membership revenue from $22,000 to $40,000 in just two years.

Graphic Artist

⇨ **Achievement:** Quickly assigned to a major corporate client by senior agency staff based on high performance.

⇨ **Scope:** Worked on small projects using digital images and 3D architectural design.

⇨ **Contribution:** Demonstrated his value with hard work and dedication.

⇨ **Outcome:** Given advanced responsibility to design and create packaging, advertisements, and sales materials for a top pharmaceutical firm.

⇨ **Final achievement statement:** Hired by ad agency to handle smaller projects using digital images and virtual 3D architectural design. Talent and strong performance quickly led to higher-level project of designing and creating packaging, advertisements, and sales materials for a top pharmaceutical firm.

Now try out SCO on one of your achievements. Remember to always start your statement with a strong action verb.

Branding

To succeed in today's innovation and gig economy, you might look at yourself as a product. This means you have to find the best way to sell yourself. For an introvert, this is not the most appealing task, but you can begin your self-promotion with your resume by creating a personal brand that is uniquely *you* and catches the prospective employer's eye. If viewing yourself as a "brand" seems cold, objectifying, and impersonal (as it will to introverts), consider the concept of resume branding as an introduction to the employer and a way to display the fuller story of your career. This perspective will help you conjure up your quiet energy and fuel your intense concentration to craft a powerfully written resume. To get you started in building your brand, let's look at a step-by-step process for writing a headline and summary.

Recent graduates or women reentering the workforce don't need to worry about branding and writing headlines. The goal is to gain experience and credibility, keeping track of your accomplishments as you go along. Similarly, if your field is academia or research, you are likely to have a CV (curriculum vitae), which doesn't require a branding statement. Your accomplishments will be reflected in your research publications and presentations.

Headline

An energetic and well-composed headline quickly heralds who you are, defines your job target, and signals what it is that makes you unique. Most important, it quickly establishes your brand. Think of the headline as setting the scene for what's to come in the most impressive parts of your resume: experiences, accomplishments, and educational background.

You already worked through your achievements, so keep that list handy. Now pull out your list of personal characteristics and skills. Consider adding to these lists specific skills relevant in your field.

Choose a general position title that fits your career background as well as your target employer. Then consider which strategy you believe to be the optimal, most dynamic choice for capturing the prospective employer's eye. As a rule, the best attention-getters include an overview of recognized accomplishments or skill sets in demand by the target employer.

Here are three examples of powerful headlines. Although each differs in style, they all provide the employer a quick glimpse of the individual as a person and valuable asset.

Human Resource Leader and Change Manager

⇨ **Headline features:** Simple and to the point. You can add more information later in your summary.

Ambitious and innovative pharmaceutical sales rep consistently recognized for exceeding sales goals and performance standards.

⇨ **Headline features:** Highlights personal qualities and accomplishments of interest to employers in corporate sales.

Business Director and Consultant
Leadership/Project Management/Process Improvement

⇨ **Headline features:** Includes multiple position titles and key management functions that would attract a targeted employer.

Summary

Most headlines are followed by a short summary, sometimes referred to as a profile. The summary supports your headline, providing career highlights, achievements, expertise, and personal characteristics that have brightly colored your success and established your brand. This is your value proposition in four to five sentences.

An easy way to break down some of the most important components of your experience is to separate them into categories and then use that information to craft a summary that supports your brand.

⇨ Career highlights: Years of experience (if relevant), knowledge, and expertise

⇨ Key atrengths and talents

⇨ Achievements

⇨ Personal characteristics

Let's take another look at our talented HR professional and see how she integrated these core components in her summary.

Human Resource Leader and Change Manager

Compassionate leader with track record of exceeding workforce goals by focusing on business priorities. Recognized for outstanding performance and awarded highest employee honor (NOVA) by the CEO for outstanding leadership to "People Transformation" across the enterprise resulting in an increase of 10 percent employee satisfaction.

Her core components break down as follows:

⇨ **Career highlight:** History of exceeding workforce goals

⇨ **Key strength:** Leadership

⇨ **Achievements:** NOVA award and increase in employee satisfaction

⇨ **Personal characteristics:** Compassionate

Now let's look at two other approaches to summaries, one by an IT professional and one by a teacher, that include the core competencies. Instead of including all of the elements in a single paragraph, these highlight certain competencies by separating them out in a different format.

Senior IT Professional

Innovative technology leader with cross-domain experience, recognized for delivering ground-up software and new process solutions. Adept at bridging the communication gap between customers, management, and technology staff. Talent for producing forward-thinking design and conceptualizing long-term vision.

Key Skills

IT Strategy and Leadership	Team Communications	Service Management
Database Design	Process Design and Improvement	Change Management
Training Development	Software Design and Development	Excel
ServiceNow	PowerPoint	SharePoint

Technology is a field in which specific skills like software and process design are extremely important. Including a separate section for skills along with the summary paragraph incorporates keywords while giving the employer a feel for the quality and strength of your technology abilities. In addition to assessing this candidate's computer competencies, a prospective employer quickly learns that this applicant has cross-domain experience, plus skills as a creative designer and problem-solver. This candidate also highlights an ability to communicate with people at all levels—another plus to employers.

Elementary School Teacher

Enthusiastic and resourceful teacher dedicated to creating an effective learning environment that meets students' social, emotional, and cognitive needs, and strives to help students achieve their full potential.

⇨ *Designed and developed innovative curriculum to accommodate different learning styles and levels.*

⇨ *Created and introduced lesson unit on multicultural awareness adopted as model learning unit in all Millersville elementary school districts.*

⇨ *Adept at providing classroom structure, discipline, and support to help children succeed academically and socially.*

⇨ *Readily establishes trusting relationships with students, teachers, administrators, and parents.*

⇨ *Elected as faculty representative to Millersville School Board.*

This educator accompanies her summary with bulleted statements to describe her philosophy and approach to teaching; these bullets also list two important achievements ("elected as faculty representative" and "introduced lesson unit on multicultural awareness") that make her stand out as a potential job candidate in her field.

Short-and-Sweet Descriptions

In your quest to do full justice to your experience, you might find yourself getting carried away with too many adjectives, taking the reader down the rabbit hole of endlessly long sentences. Resist this temptation, and give the prospective employer what they really want: a down-to-earth feel for what you do on a daily basis. If you are a consultant or business owner, customers and clients need a reliable understanding of your services and how they can use them.

With the constant barrage of information from cyberspace, modern-day employers primarily focus on your results and achievements. So, avoid cluttering your resume; use space economically to describe the most basic tasks in your job description. Before you start to write, clear your mind of the mass of material your psyche wants to relay, and edit this down to what you know is most relevant to the audience. Then organize your resume by crafting a clear, easily digested description of your key responsibilities and tasks. Once you have written a description of a job, follow it up with your bullet list of achievements. Finally, always begin a description with a strong action verb, and avoid the phrase "duties/responsibilities include."

Here are some examples of powerful, short-and-sweet sentences that highlight a key responsibility:

⇨ Lead and manage team of six account representatives in developing dynamic partnerships with more than fifty hospitals and cancer centers across Maryland.

⇨ Assessed business requirements and defined and implemented solutions capitalizing on both offshore and onshore resources.

⇨ Conceptualized and wrote previews and columns for NHL, MLB, and college sports released to national and international outlets.

Keywords

As you craft your resume, keep in mind that employers and recruiters are using computer sourcing and tracking systems these days to rapidly scan resumes and LinkedIn profiles. Keywords are the specific words or phrases employers use to find the right candidate among the multitudes of applicants. To ensure that you are noticed in the whirling world of recruiting, your resume should brim with these industry buzzwords.

Let's take a look at an effective list of keywords provided by a registered hospital nurse in the skills section of her resume:

⇨ Emergency Procedures

⇨ Life Support

⇨ ICU

⇨ CCU

⇨ Intravenous Therapy

⇨ Care Plan Administration

⇨ Charting and Documenting

⇨ Community Health Issues

⇨ Physician Relations

One of the best strategies for identifying keywords is to peruse job postings on job websites and LinkedIn as these are often loaded with industry-specific buzzwords. Save or print out three similar job postings. As you read through the job descriptions, you will notice a pattern of similar keywords, providing clues to which keywords you should incorporate into your resume. Using word clouds like Wordle.net or TagCrowd.com is another fun, visual way to find elusive keywords in job descriptions. Simply copy and paste a job description into the word cloud, and a cloud of words appears in a colorful design, giving greater prominence to words that appear more frequently in the posting. Jobscan is a new and excellent tool for resume optimization.

Education and Other Valuable Categories

Listing your degrees, majors, and educational institutions is essential, but don't stop there. If you are a recent bachelor or master's degree graduate, consider listing coursework, a research project, or a senior capstone project that's relevant to your job target. You can also include scholarships awarded and special honors. GPA can be a sensitive issue for some, but if you are proud of yours and consider it a major accomplishment, proudly display it under the education category.

If you have been out of school for five or more years, the education heading and supportive information should appear toward the end of your resume. Employers are most interested in what you are doing currently, so experience should be one of the first categories they see on your resume. Those who earned an advanced degree (MBA, RN, PhD, JD, etc.) should include the degree initials next to their name.

If you are a recent PhD grad looking for career options beyond academia, include on your resume the specific presentations and publications relevant to your job target. This eliminates the need to attach a complete, lengthy list from an academic CV.

The acceleration of change in the workplace will continue to demand lifelong learning, and you can demonstrate that you possess this enviable gem by polishing up and showing off any additional professional or academic training you have received. If you completed supplementary coursework or earned a professional certificate, these are assets and can be included under the "Education" heading, too. Gaining special training like Six Sigma or sharpening technology skills is yet another way to underline your success in remaining relevant and up-to-date in your field.

As an introvert, you may overlook the value of enriching your resume with other categories that could sway an employer in your direction. This might include a wide array of potential areas demonstrating your merits, from awards and professional affiliations, to community service, publications, and more.

Honors/Awards

If you are a student or recent graduate with a strong academic record or other valuable feathers in your cap, wave these achievements with both hands. Did you win an award for exceeding sales quotas, introduce a sustainability program, or come up with a strategy to streamline costs? Make it flash on your resume.

Professional Affiliations

Someone who regularly updates their professional knowledge and sharpens their skills understandably impresses employers. If you have served on a committee or been elected officer of a professional association, say so loud and clear. Don't make it difficult for employers to find phrases that clearly say, "I am a leader!"

Presentations/Public Speaking Engagements

Your ability to communicate ideas or knowledge in today's information-hungry workplace is in great demand. Use your resume to show employers you can promote your knowledge and organizational goals in front of groups—without fear of public speaking. If you have presented reports, workshops, or training either in person or via webinars, these activities are a big plus and should be added to your resume. Sure, you are an introvert, but never discount your public speaking skills.

Community Service/Volunteering

Examples of good citizenship reassure an employer that a prospective employee is a harmonious team player. Being active in your community increases the chances that you'll work collaboratively with colleagues and accept supervisory direction and advice. The workplace may own you from nine to five, but you represent the company in a real sense after hours. When you serve on community boards or volunteer for a worthy cause, you enhance your value to the organization.

Publications

Publishing professional articles or research studies in your field demonstrate your writing and editing talents, skills valued by many employers. It is also through publishing that your knowledge and expertise reaches a national audience, which is another appealing aspect to an employer. Online publications and blogs similarly increase your visibility and should be highlighted in this category, too.

Visual Presentation

Job hunters are often anxious for employers to notice their most impressive experience, so the resume's overall presentation does not receive much attention. Don't make this mistake; select an appealing format and eye-catching layout to make your resume stand out from the others.

Use these tips as guidelines to get you started. Just make sure you follow the two key rules of layout and format: design a resume that's visually appealing, and make sure it's easy to read.

⇨ **Times New Roman works fine,** but don't be timid about creating some flair with something more elegant. Several other fonts are appealing to the eye and convert well in attachments, such as Garamond, Arial, Georgia, Helvetica, and Calibri. Although these fonts are some of the most popular, there is no need to limit yourself to these styles. Particularly if your field is in the arts or visual design, try going with something fancier.

⇨ **Use bold type and italics, varying font size, and uppercase lettering for accent,** luring the attention of the reader to information that best reveals who you are. Take note, however, that italics are quirky to the eye, so avoid overuse, especially where you wish to provide detailed information.

⇨ **Keep font size between 10 and 12 points,** depending on the style of choice. Resist the temptation to use more than two fonts in any one resume, as the reader may become blurry-eyed, and therefore stop reading it entirely.

⇨ **Consider adding a pop of color,** if you are adventurous. Or go conservative: gray, light blue, or pale beige are examples of softer resume color choices. If you prefer to be bold, red can work well, too; alternatively, avoid shades too bright or too light. Try out color with one design element, such as main headings or shading for lines under headings or contact information. And of course there is nothing wrong with the conventional black and white.

⇨ **Add a graph or chart** for eye-catching results that draw attention to business, revenue, or sales growth. Your skills and special achievements can also stand out with a smart-looking graphic. Microsoft Word and a variety of other computer programs offer an attractive selection of user-friendly graph and chart templates.

⇨ **Bold your name and main headings** to give your resume visual definition.

⇨ **Eliminate your street address** if you are concerned about confidentiality and safety issues. Be sure to include your phone number and email address, and it's not a bad idea to include the URL to your LinkedIn profile.

⇨ **Balance the information visually on the page,** making sure you have enough white space versus text.

⇨ **Bullets that pinpoint achievement and target skills** are easy to follow, but keep in mind that overly lengthy lists can be exhausting to the eye and therefore counterproductive.

⇨ **Be consistent in your approach** to your visual layout so the reader can easily identify a pattern.

⇨ **Avoid Word templates.** They tend to restrict your creativity and fail to reflect your individuality. These templates can also make it difficult to make any format changes.

Before you release it for public view, always print out your resume, proofread carefully, and place yourself in the prospective employer's shoes: Is it visually inviting and reader friendly? Also, don't be penny wise and pound foolish; always use a higher grade of paper—never plain copy paper—as you will bring a hard copy of your resume to interviews, job fairs, and network meetings.

Send Your Resume Into Cyberspace

Once your resume is ready, you want to be sure the potential employer receives it. Keep the following suggestions in mind to ensure your resume reaches its destinations snag free.

Upload Your Resume

Most of today's employers require that you send your resume as an attachment to a specific email address or upload it to a website. This may require small edits or changes in format. Follow the employer's instructions on uploading your resume to ensure the document is readable. Save your resume in both Word and PDF files, and check to make sure it is loaded with job-related keywords.

Applicant Tracking Systems (ATS)

Employers in many large companies and recruiting firms now use time-saving and money-saving ATS or computer-sourcing systems to quickly scan resumes and identify top candidates. Because formatting errors can deliver a one-punch knockout as you compete for attention in these tracking systems, be sure to use a plain, ATS-friendly version of your resume. Studies show that nearly 75 percent of applicants are rejected through ATS due to submitting an overly stylized format.[2]

To steer clear of these formatting issues when applying to large companies, keep your documents simple and clean by following these basic suggestions.

⇨ Attach documents in RTF or Word files; avoid using PDF files, which don't read well for ATS systems.

⇨ Use common headings like "Summary," "Skills," "Professional Experience," and "Education."

⇨ Avoid tables, graphs, or any fancy symbols.

⇨ Use standard font styles.

⇨ Bullets are okay, but avoid arrows and check marks.

⇨ Stay away from shading and borders.

⇨ Save your resume, preferably using your last name and the word "resume" in the title.

And just a reminder: Keywords are key in an ATS-friendly resume.

You can often determine which employers use ATS systems by going to the "Careers/Jobs" page on the company website. An ATS vendor logo may appear at the bottom of the page. If you don't see any of this branding, move your mouse over the "Apply" button and check the browser window. You are likely to see the destination URL. If the company is using ATS, the URL domain will indicate the vendor.

Keep in mind that most people find opportunities through referrals and connections. When a hiring manager reaches out based on a referral, this confirms that all the time and energy you expended writing and designing an eye-catching resume was worth it. You won't be sending that resume through a cold tracking system; rather, your contact will hand deliver it to the hiring manager, or you will attach the resume as a Word or PDF file to an email address.

When it comes to one-on-one networking meetings or potential business opportunities, a resume with substantive content and an appealing design serves as a marketing centerpiece. And don't let a pending interview find you without a hard copy of your resume in hand.

PROMOTE YOURSELF IN REAL TIME

The tentacles of social media may seem threatening from an introvert's point of view. You prefer to retain your privacy, so you may be concerned about overexposure online. In today's competitive market, however, you must be ready and willing to expose a portion of your private self to join the online ranks of other successful professionals. If you are still feeling apprehensive, don't turn the page quite yet. Even an introvert like yourself can learn to open the door just enough to make social media an effective and amiable tool.

Using social media allows you to put quality thought into building your brand and establishing an attractive online presence. Not only does social media give you time to think before you write, but you can sit at your desk and quietly research and review company summaries without interruption. At the same time, this platform lets you reach out and establish valuable professional contacts.

In this chapter I will demonstrate how social media is a perfect marketing tool for introverts. I will help you determine the optimal level of exposure to support your professional development while respecting your need for adequate privacy. You will learn to write a complete and engaging

professional profile on LinkedIn as well as shorter profiles for Twitter and
Facebook. And you'll be wide-eyed with amazement when you realize the
extent to which social media can complement and support your working
life.

LinkedIn

LinkedIn has become one of the most powerful forces in the career-
building cosmos. This essential tool is an ideal way to connect with
industry professionals, and it paves the way along a smooth, fast track to
exploring and identifying new opportunities. As of this writing, LinkedIn has 575 million national and international members representing
200 countries. Considering it has190 million users a day and three million active job leads, an ever-growing cadre of hiring managers and recruiters look to LinkedIn as a strong ally to find winning candidates.[1]

Let the Force of LinkedIn Be With You

With half a billion members, LinkedIn is the largest online professional
network. It has many benefits, some of which are included in the following
list. LinkedIn:

⇨ **Increases visibility.** You can find people, and people can find
  you. This is the beauty of LinkedIn for introverts. Since you have
  already introduced yourself in writing through your profile, a
  prospective employer or colleague can easily locate you and learn
  more about your professional background, accomplishments, and
  skills before contacting you about a potential opportunity. Alternatively, if you are reaching out to a colleague or senior leader you
  haven't personally met, you avoid telephone tag and voicemail
  messages—another plus for introverts. On LinkedIn you make the
  initial connection by sending an introductory message through
  your profile, which could get you a quicker response than traditional voicemail messaging.

⇨ **Builds networks.** The very heart of LinkedIn is the capability it
  provides to build and organize your professional network. You

can easily invite people to join your network, and an invitee just might lead you to a valuable contact.

⇨ **Provides up-to-date information.** LinkedIn is a terrific resource on so many levels. You can get continuing updates on what is happening behind the scenes in your field. You can also accept invitations to join groups, as well as research summaries of companies and organizations that interest you.

⇨ **Maximizes job postings.** More and more employers are flocking to LinkedIn to advertise job openings. Recruiters and hiring managers have made it their quest to pinpoint a champion candidate by scanning hundreds of LinkedIn profiles.

⇨ **Enhances opportunity.** LinkedIn can also lead to offers for contract work on special projects, a request for a speaking engagement, or an opportunity to write for blogs or publications.

You might feel as if the whole world is watching you on social media. This is the reason introverts often turn on the caution light and offer minimal information on their profiles. Whatever your reservations are, don't take the nearest exit. Give yourself the green light to discover what LinkedIn can offer you, and create a profile that will get noticed by colleagues, employers, and leaders in your field.

Robert: The LinkedIn Doubter

When Robert, a reserved but fully competent introvert, initially hopped on the LinkedIn bandwagon, he set up his account to include the bare minimum about his experience and skills. After I explained how he could leverage LinkedIn in his career, Robert decided to go the distance with his profile. We worked on expanding his LinkedIn summary and opening the door to more contacts.

As a result, a rich and unexpected opportunity developed when his former boss, Suzanne, a vice provost of student affairs, accepted his invitation to connect. She sent him a LinkedIn message suggesting they catch up over the phone. They spoke soon thereafter, discussing new trends and trajectories they were seeing in the field. Suzanne then told Robert she had been invited to present a workshop at a major professional conference and asked Robert to be her coleader. This is a classic and compelling example of how a LinkedIn connection can directly lead to an exciting opportunity.

Stepping Into LinkedIn

Getting started on LinkedIn is simple! Follow these steps and you'll have an attractive and exciting account in no time.

Open an Account

Simply go to the website, fill out some basic information, and click the "Join" button. You will be asked to confirm your email. Don't worry about how you come across on LinkedIn just yet; you can decide when to make your information public.

Choose a Headshot

Your photo is one of the first things people see when they view your profile. Make sure you look approachable and professional in your picture. Think of your photo as a means to convey personal qualities such as warmth, seriousness, and compassion. Although approximately 60 percent of the photo is your face, dress in a way that matches your industry and professional level. If you are still wavering about including a photo, think again. According to recent LinkedIn statistics, views of your profile increase by eleven times when you include a headshot.

Write a Headline

Say your headline out loud, as this is the first line of text that appears at the top right-hand side beneath your name. You can use the headline from your resume as a starting point, but you may want to tweak and adjust the text to generate more electricity and overall appeal.

Let's look at four headline examples that use different styles and approaches to successfully target their industry.

Chief Creative Officer
Strategist on storytelling, development, and execution—a "show whisperer" to media producers and content networks.

Customer Success Manager: *Empowering Customers to Excel at Social Selling*

Veterinarian, Feline Medicine and Surgery

Experienced Criminal Defense and Civil Rights Attorney

To attract clients and customers, the first two examples include tag lines that explain their functions in greater depth. In contrast, the last two represent more conventional fields and therefore focus their headlines on their areas of expertise without additional commentary.

Summarize Your Information

This is where the overture plays and the curtain goes up on you and your career, so turn a spotlight on yourself that brings colleagues and prospective employers to their feet with applause. As you do with a resume, consider the characteristics and needs of the target audience, and weave those all-important keywords into the fabric of your summary. You can borrow from your resume summary here, but remember that you have 2,000 characters in a LinkedIn profile. This reality gives you more space to create a self-portrait that shines.

To get a jump on writing your LinkedIn summary, answer the following questions. You might not use all the information from your answers, but thinking about these questions will help you determine what to pinpoint in your summary.

⇨ What are the central themes of your career story?

⇨ What makes you a competent professional?

⇨ What are your most significant career achievements? (You should already have some answers to this question from Chapter 3.)

⇨ What compliments have you received from supervisors, colleagues, customers, or clients about your work and personal style?

⇨ In which areas do you have professional expertise?

⇨ How have you have built and sustained professional relationships?

⇨ In which industry databases, programs, tools, or techniques are you proficient?

The following examples present different styles of LinkedIn summaries. However, they all succeed in telling a more vivid career story than the summary written for a resume, and their use of the first person brings out a personal, engaging tone.

Technology Consultant

IT and Change Professional | Connecting People, Ideas, and Technology

I believe technology that embraces human factors can make peoples' lives better. But often when change is necessary, people respond with skepticism.

I focus my talents and creative curiosity on inspiring and empowering people to thrive throughout the change process. Management appreciates my people-centered approach, leveraging the powerful affinity between the principles of user experience and those of change management. Because in the end, it is the people *who are affected most by new systems, websites, or products.*

Susan uses the summary to introduce her philosophy on technology and how it impacts people. Her purpose and personality come through as well as her approach to working with her senior-level clients. This summary is creative and engaging.

Director at Open Book

Writing and Publishing Consultant/Entrepreneur

I spent my career in the publishing industry as an editor, literary agent, journalist, and author. I am a creative thinker and problem-solver, and I love to innovate. My favorite phrase is: "I have an idea!" I'm a skilled writer and editor, and enjoy helping authors make their writing better. I've written and published several books and currently write a regular blog, "Get Lit," for Philadelphia City Paper. *I also run a new independent bookstore, The Open Book Bookstore.*

This summary combines a variety of roles and skills with achievements and personality, all powerfully packed into a single paragraph.

COO, Liveoak Technologies

I am currently the Chief Operating Officer at Liveoak Technologies. This startup combines video-conferencing, real-time collaboration, and electronic signature to help enterprises better serve their customers and eliminate paperwork. I lead Liveoak's NYC presence and focus on sales and business development.

Most recently, I was a Program Associate with the Barclays Accelerator powered by Techstars. Prior to Techstars, I was an Investment Banking Associate in the Real Estate Group at Credit Suisse. I have experience analyzing and executing IPOs, M&A, and other capital markets trans-actions for REITs, hotels, homebuilders, casinos, and leisure companies. Prior to joining Credit Suisse, I received a JD/MBA from Vanderbilt University and a BA from Duke University.

I'm an open networker—I can be reached at: jjjjjjj@gmail.com

This young professional uses his summary as a focal point for his experience, skill set, qualifications, and overall credibility. Like many young professionals, he has already had more than one career. Emphasizing his experience and qualifications works well in the summary because it supports the trajectory and diversity of his career.

These examples demonstrate that it is possible, within your own comfort level and style, to compose a summary that stands proud, recognizes the qualities that make you unique and valuable, and supports your brand. When composing your summary, first consider the nature of your industry and your career background. Next, envision how these blend with your distinctive talents and personal strengths. Then it is up to you to decide how best to use all of this seminal information to score big points on your LinkedIn summary.

Skill Set

Listing skills on your profile page is easy! Pull from the skills exercise and from your resume, and people will see how competent and knowledgeable you are. If you still find yourself struggling to identify some important skills related to your field, go to *www.linkedin.com/directory/topics-a/* and look up job titles or general industry areas; there you will see a list of the top skills associated with each job title. Add the ones that genuinely reflect your abilities to the list of skills on your profile. An added benefit to listing skills: They are often rich in keywords, which can further attract recruiters and hiring managers who use computer systems to track candidates.

Once you complete your list, you open the door for colleagues and professional contacts to endorse your skills. Of course, you will want to reciprocate and endorse your contacts for their skills, too.

Recommendations

Don't be bashful when it comes to something as "self-serving" as asking for recommendations. If you excelled at your work, allow others the honor of acknowledging your success. Recognize that bosses or clients are usually delighted to give you that deserved pat on the back and validate your star performance.

If you are an entrepreneur or if you work in fields such as consulting or marketing and sales, seek recommendations from customers or clients. Recommendations back up and support the hard-earned accomplishments and rich attributes that you present in your profile.

Many senior-level professionals are now accustomed to writing short recommendations for employees or clients on LinkedIn, which tend to be a total of four to five sentences. This is far less demanding than writing the longer, traditional letters of recommendation. Think strategically and select a mix of people who can speak about different skills and achievements. Depending on your relationship with the person, you may even want to offer some pointers on what to emphasize. If you receive a recommendation that is poorly written or you don't feel comfortable with, don't worry. LinkedIn will forward the recommendation to you first via email, and you can decide whether or not you want to accept it. Rest assured that a recommendation is never posted on your profile without your permission.

After you review a recommendation, you may see a spelling error or a slight problem with the content. If you feel comfortable doing so, you can request that the person make small edits or changes on a LinkedIn recommendation.

Consider paying it forward. As others have done for you, be willing to write LinkedIn recommendations for colleagues, interns, or employees you have mentored, supervised, or highly respect.

Accomplishments

Consider adding some accomplishments, such as certifications, community involvement, volunteer experiences, academic course work, publications, and any honors bestowed and awards presented. Just as these features enhance your resume, they also champion your success on your LinkedIn profile.

Education

Similar to a resume, this profile includes the basics of your academic background: your college or university, major, and degree. You can also use this section to list school activities, academic societies, research study, or special projects (if you are a recent graduate). If you have been out of school for a while but continue your involvement in alumni activities, you can highlight this as well. It's also fine to leave out graduation dates if you finished school many years ago and are sensitive to age discrimination.

Groups

LinkedIn Groups are taking flight as an ever-increasing array of professions and industries have organized them. Imagine these groups as a dynamic constellation of stars in your field from all over the professional galaxy. These groups allow you to widen your world to the entire planet. You can participate in relevant industry discussions with other group members and discover resources to support your career development.

This is an industrial-strength network tool for introverts. Just by tapping your keyboard, you can build rewarding and productive relationships with experts in your field and remain on the cutting-edge of your profession—not to mention the added benefit of colleagues, hiring managers, and senior leaders in your field noticing that you are serious about your professional development.

Multimedia and Video

Make a head-turning splash on your LinkedIn profile by sprinkling in some media. Have you created and presented a slide show at work or managed a special event? How about that article you wrote for a professional online publication? Or maybe you hit the big time with a piece published by popular online media like the *Huffington Post*. What about the valuable advice you provided on your blog? Put a spotlight on your career story in words and pictures with the artful use of multimedia posts in your profile. Just hit the edit pencil in the uppermost section of your profile, and you will see the "Media" heading. Here you can either upload a file or add a link to videos, photos, external documents (such as articles), or presentations (such as slides).

If you can let go of some modesty, include a video clip that shows you delivering a presentation to a group. Or be daring and produce a three-minute video showing off your knowledge and passion for the work you do. Whether you prefer to display your writing talent while staying discreetly behind the scenes, or you present a video clip and go boldly where you've never gone before, multimedia can help you tell your story in brazen and brilliant color.

Tie a Bow on Your LinkedIn Profile

⇨ **Customize your URL:** When you sign up, LinkedIn provides you with a URL that includes a chunk of numbers alongside your name. Since you will use this LinkedIn URL to promote your profile on your resume and business cards, you'll want to keep it as simple as possible. To simplify your URL address to the user friendly LinkedIn.com/yourname, just click "edit" and get rid of all the numbers.

⇨ **Add links:** You can include up to three URLs on your profile summary. Links to your professional website, blog, or online portfolio can supplement your profile and further demonstrate your technical and work-related skills.

⇨ **Include relevant job descriptions:** It isn't necessary to list every job you have ever held under the "Experience" category. Include jobs that match your career goals and target employers, and describe the most relevant parts of your experience. You can paste in some descriptions from your resume, but make these shorter and tighter on LinkedIn. If you have been out of work for a while or recently graduated, it is perfectly acceptable to list internships and volunteer and leadership activities. Keep in mind your readers' mad dash to review your profile; if it starts to feel like a never-ending journey, you will lose their attention and patience.

⇨ **Update your status:** Check in frequently with your LinkedIn profile to make sure your information is current and up to date. Post updates on any changes that may have occurred in your professional life, such as a job change or promotion, industry awards, or a special achievement.

⇨ **Stay on top of your game:** Make an effort to post and share industry-related articles or questions that might provoke an energetic discussion at least once or twice a month. In addition, be vigilant about reading posts from colleagues or leaders. When you discover a colleague has posted an update about a promotion or new job, be sure to congratulate them! And don't miss the possibility of colleagues, employers, and recruiters reaching out to you through LinkedIn email messages. An exciting new opportunity or a connection with a thought leader could be waiting for you.

⇨ **Indicate your "Career Interests":** As recruiters scan LinkedIn for candidates, they may identify you as a top contender. However, they don't know whether you are genuinely interested in a new opportunity, which can be a waste of their time. If you are not actively seeking a new job but are open to possibilities and opportunities, take a look at LinkedIn's "Career Interests" feature, highlighted under the "Jobs" search function. Here you may fill out information about your job position preferences, titles, industry interests, and desirable geographic region. Completing this will satisfy recruiters and hiring managers as to whether you are genuinely open to new horizons. At the same time, you can rest easy that your professional intentions will not be exposed to the entire universe.

Linked In Connections: Contacts and More Contacts

LinkedIn "connections" inject fuel into your profile by helping you build a dynamic professional network. Remember: Potential career opportunities grow exponentially as your network spreads further and further. After all, how often you have heard stories about someone who found a new job, landed a promotion, or secured work on a special project because they knew an important contact at the organization? Think of LinkedIn as the engine that can power and drive these connections.

A robust list of contacts also shows the professional world that you exist and are committed to building a flourishing network of achievers. The last thing you want to do is send a message to colleagues and potential employers that you fear social media and are half-hearted about engaging with other professionals. You don't need to have 500-plus contacts to feel popular, but a base of fifty to 125 connections is a realistic starting point. It is certainly okay to maintain some privacy in your life, but don't live in a cocoon on LinkedIn. As you meet colleagues and senior leaders at conferences, training sessions, and even in the social stream of life, follow up by sending them a friendly invitation to "connect" on LinkedIn.

LinkedIn Identity: Your Essential Online Presence

Not all employers use LinkedIn to formally recruit candidates. But they are likely to Google you to check out your online presence. Since LinkedIn has a high SEO ranking, your profile will be one of the first links that appears on any Google search. Therefore, whether they are regular LinkedIn users or not, the vast majority of employers will at least peek at your profile.

Recently, I served as board member on a search committee of a small nonprofit organization that was looking for a new executive director. The committee posted the open position on LinkedIn and also on local non-profit websites. Strong candidates came forth quickly and eagerly. First, we Googled the top candidates to assess the quality and content of their professional profile on LinkedIn. The few that neglected to establish a LinkedIn profile, we quickly eliminated. The committee unanimously felt that any viable candidate would recognize the power of LinkedIn to promote an organization, reach out to colleagues, support professional development, and provide a hiring tool to find the most competent staff. Most important, such a candidate would know how to maximize the potential of this essential tool to achieve all of those things for our organization.

People still find jobs, make network connections, and advance their careers without the direct benefit of LinkedIn. But in cyberspace, if you are not on LinkedIn, you don't exist on a professional level.

Twitter

Do I have to tweet, too? With 328 million monthly users, Twitter is a social networking tool that informs readers of your actions and opinions at any given moment.[2] I can hear your introverted voice saying, "Whoa! I never signed up to have my life on the front page." Relax. Tweeting allows you to choose when and to whom you want to tweet, so you can easily safeguard your need for privacy.

What differentiates Twitter from LinkedIn is that it's an open network. On LinkedIn, you and your contact agree to be connected. However, if someone follows you on Twitter, you don't have to follow him or her back. You can read tweets by senior leaders, experts, or authors in your field without being officially connected to them. So why not be bold and tweet a question to an industry expert or show interest by responding to a colleague's tweet?

Twitter in Real Time

If you are new to this social network, you can start out by following thought leaders or colleagues. Then you can begin sending tweets (short blurbs of 280 characters) that demonstrate your industry knowledge and insight, or pose questions that spark a tweet response. If you are at a conference listening to a keynote speech by a well-respected leader in your field, you can tweet and share any inspiration or wisdom you have gained in real time. One of the more popular career-driven ways to use this popular network is to tweet an industry-related article or blog post, or provoke a discussion. Twitter automatically shortens these links to allow the URL to fit into your tweet.

Hashtags

A unique feature of Twitter is the use of hashtags. Using the hashtag symbol # before a word or short phrase in your tweet will transform it into a searchable link. For example, if you are looking for opportunities in New York, you might use #jobs #NYC in your tweet to find job postings in the area or join a conversation on a particular topic. You can also click on a hashtag like #careeradvice to see other twitter posts on this topic. Alternatively, you might use hashtags to find thought leaders in your field or jump into an industry conversation. In a word, hashtags help clarify your tweet and organize content on your Twitter thread.

The Twitter Profile

Creating a profile on Twitter is a lot less cumbersome than on LinkedIn. Just go to Twitter.com, fill out the following information, and you are set to go.

⇨ **Name and handle (@name):** This is your identifying information. A good rule of thumb for your Twitter handle is to use your full name (@GretaNavarro). If you are on Twitter to promote a product or service, use the business name for your Twitter handle (@CapTech). Your business or full name will appear above your handle.

⇨ **Photo:** If you are satisfied with your LinkedIn photo, go ahead and use it for Twitter, too. Keep in mind that every tweet you send will include your photo, so make sure it is a flattering image. If you are promoting a business, you can also upload your logo. Always remember that your photo or logo is representing your brand.

⇨ **Header background:** Think of this as a billboard for your bio, so introduce a creative touch with a well-chosen photo or eye-appealing graphic that marries well with your brand. If your taste veers toward the conservative, simply select a bright color for your background. You might also check out sites like Snappa.com or Canva.com that offer free designs you can customize.

⇨ **Bio:** The Twitter bio resembles a short advertisement. You have 160 characters to encapsulate what it is that makes you unique and would create a following among other tweeters. It's optional, but you can personalize the bio by adding some treasured interests and career highlights. This is also the place to include a link to your website or blog.

Check out the following three examples to get an idea of an appealing Twitter bio.

Media strategist; consults on content, development, storytelling, and audience strategies; frequent speaker, panelist, and Northwestern grad program adjunct

This bio quickly spells out the tweeter's main role as media strategist and areas of expertise.

Customer Success@LinkedIn.com I'm passionate about technology, healthy living & learning new things.

This example mixes professional background with some of the tweeter's compelling interests.

Fashion designer and fiber artist whose passion is one-of-a-kind, show-stopping coats for men and women.

Even artists tweet. After reading this short bio, don't you want to buy a coat?

If you are struggling with how to properly articulate who you are in your bio, go back to your resume headline and summary or LinkedIn summary for inspiration. Let's take a look at how one client transformed his resume headline and summary into a Twitter bio

Research Sociologist, Senior Social Science, and Health Policy Researcher

Resume Summary

Expert in data analysis, research, and translating findings into popular, professional, and policy-oriented forums. Skillful at using administrative datasets as a basis for identifying and improving outcomes for services to homeless and related populations.

Twitter Bio

Homelessness researcher @HSS.gov; consultant; recovering professor. PhD sociology alum @SociologyAtHarvard, policy wonk, and urban guy.

The resume summary is a more formal description of experience that includes some salient keywords such as "data analysis," "data sets," "outcomes," and "homelessness." The Twitter bio, on the other hand, provides a snapshot of the subject's professional and educational background, but incorporates more informal terms such as "policy wonk" and "urban guy."

To Tweet or Not to Tweet

To better determine whether Twitter would be a useful tool for you, let's review some of its benefits. First—and this is a plus for the job hunter—recruiters often post a number of jobs on Twitter before they are officially advertised on the boards. Second, it is easy to set up a Twitter account, assuring that you receive job postings in real time. Third, if you are a business owner, Twitter is a proven and powerful machine for generating new business leads. If your strategy is just to stay on top of your game, Twitter will be a great friend in introducing you to colleagues and leaders in your field.

If you are still in a twitter about using Twitter, hashtag your field to see who is actively tweeting, and take note of which topics are being discussed. For example, if you are a biomedical engineer, search under #biomedicalengineer, and you will find two professional societies and Twitter posts that include topics on innovation, current research, job opportunities, and upcoming conferences. If you find the subjects of these posts relevant and interesting, this would be a good indication that Twitter will be a good addition to your social media toolbox.

Facebook

If you have any doubt that Facebook is the overwhelming favorite social media site in the world, consider the fact that it has close to two billion active users a month.[3] This places Facebook at the top of the standings in the social networking major leagues.

Facebook users connect with family and friends to share life vignettes and photos, exchange stories, tell tales of thousands of words with videos, and give their opinion on political and social issues. Because Facebook is so powerful, it is advisable to carefully review your profile to determine your comfort level. You will be on display to professional contacts and employers, but you maintain control over how much of your Facebook page they see. By adjusting the privacy setting for your account (click "Settings" under the drop-down menu arrow at the top right of the screen; then click "Privacy" to see your options), you can easily censure the information that "non-friends" are able to view.

For business owners that need to build their brand and eagerly seek avenues to promote their products and services, Facebook is a friend indeed. A Facebook business page allows you to post events and company advertisements, while offering a feature that enables users to buy products directly on the page. It also facilitates managing customer or client interaction as they hit the like button or engage in message exchanges.

Facebook's job boards have also become a wildly popular haunt for job hunters. Indeed (general), USAJobs (government), and coolworks (opportunities to work in resort areas), along with CareerCast and Flexjobs, are among the top job boards on Facebook. CareerCast is loaded with career and job search resources, ranking the best and worst jobs, while posting jobs in a variety of fields and industries. If you are a gig worker or interested in pursuing part-time opportunities, Flexjobs is a Facebook job board with opportunities for telecommuting, freelance, part-time, and flex schedules in many different fields.

The Facebook Profile

The process of opening a Facebook account is not much different from that of Twitter or LinkedIn. Go to Facebook.com, confirm your email, and fill out a quick form. Once you are registered, you will be led through a series of easy steps to add a personal touch to your page. Optional inclusions are educational institutions attended and employer's company name.

⇨ **Profile photo:** Despite the name "Facebook," a headshot is not required, so it's fine to opt for a more casual photo. If you prefer, choose a relaxed image that includes family or pets or presents you in a favorite setting. Using the privacy settings, you decide who sees your posts and other personal information on the page; your photo, however, is visible to all, so make sure it expresses your personality and represents who you truly are. Business owners also have the option of using their company logo, an impactful and elegant strategy in lieu of the more personal photo.

⇨ **Cover photo:** Similar to Twitter's header background, the cover photo on Facebook is larger and appears above your profile photo. Be selective and choose a graphic or photo that blends well with your profile photo and enhances the presentation of your personality.

Facebook Friends: Your Search for Connections

Once you settle on an appealing visual design, dive in and invite friends. Facebook will assist you by searching your email addresses; you can choose the friends you want to connect with and gently ignore those you do not. You can also find friends by clicking on your high school or college, or colleagues at your current or past employer under your profile. You might also enjoy clicking on your hometown or joining a regional network.

Although your main goal on Facebook may be primarily social, don't discount the possibility that your friends could have valuable professional connections. Like many mottos, the old saying "It's who you know" is true and may lead to a new professional opportunity or job.

Additional Social Media

As if LinkedIn, Twitter, and Facebook didn't give you enough social media options, you can consider a few more depending on your particular career or personal interests.

Pinterest

Imagine looking at a bulletin board at a community center or health club where thumbtacks attach a combination of photos, announcements, and notes. Pinterest is a highly visual platform with approximately 175 million members. Instead of thumbtacks, you pin images virtually to your Pinterest board.[4] It works especially well for photographers, graphic artists, and a variety of artisans who pin their creations for the world to see.

Pinterest is also ideal for marketing a product or business. Pinning colorful photos with graphics that display your products and services can give them special appeal and will increase the chance of attracting potential clients and customers. With Pinterest, you can design a board with lively images that make it pop. Then, you can use colorful tones and shades that showcase your product or services with panache and offer a glimpse into the company culture. Another dynamic feature is the "Call to Action" function. An excellent means of potential customer expansion, this feature offers your audience options such as Free Trial, Sign Up (newsletter), or Join Now. In sum, Pinterest recommends that your company board be "helpful, beautiful, and actionable," and with the help of their tools, you can achieve this goal.

You can also have fun designing a uniquely stylized resume or special work project, experimenting with colors and graphics as you pin away. Creating boards that show your previous places of work or organizations that have benefitted from your volunteer spirit can catch the employer's eye—at once sparking interest and providing information that connects with their needs. Although Pinterest is not the be-all and end-all for social media recruiting, it can be useful when you link it to your LinkedIn profile. When prospective employers scan your profile and open your Pinterest board, they view a person of talent, creativity, and experience.

If you are looking for a new opportunity, Pinterest hosts its own job boards like CareerBliss (for general advice and job search) and 405 Club (the self-named "Official Unemployed Pinboard").

Blogs

Introverts tend to focus on thoughts and ideas before ever putting them into writing (or "putting pen to paper," as we said in pre-digital days). There is no need to go against nature and compete with the more talkative and action-oriented extroverts. Instead, take advantage of your observations and well-plumbed thoughts by writing an industry-focused blog sprinkled with your innate talent and knowledge. Remaining your genuine self in your familiar, comfortable space, you can reach out to a large audience and impact social media with a gentle bang.

There are many reasons to start a blog. Are you an expert in your field? Do you want to reach multiple channels to help build your business? Is there a professional topic you are passionate about? Blogging can boost your visibility, increasing the chances that your knowledge, products, or services will be right at eye level on the shelf. An ideal medium for introverts, a blog can give you a powerful voice without speaking a word.

Regardless of where you are in your job search, the following steps can help you get started.

⇨ **Establish your audience:** When starting a blog, step one is determining your target audience. Next, speak with colleagues or survey current customers to pinpoint issues, challenges, and trends that seem universal. This will help you identify topics of interest for potential articles—subjects that will resonate with your readers.

⇨ **Choose a name:** Select a name for your blog that connects with your topic so readers will quickly identify the subject of your blog. Search online to be sure that you are not duplicating an already existing title, and then pick one that fits. If you are a business or promoting a product, simply use the company name to draw clients and customers. Many companies and organizations have linked their blogs to their websites.

⇨ **Get online:** To get your blog up and running, select a hosting and software package. Wordpress is user friendly and one of the most popular platforms. Some others include: Blogger.com, Typepad.com, and Google+. You might also ask friends and colleagues who blog for recommendations on hosting packages.

⇨ **Create a striking design:** Your goal is to create a blog that is visually attractive and has presence. Certainly, keep your blog's topic in mind, but a simple design usually works best; for interest, throw in a splash of color or a graphic. Consider an illustrative look that uses photographs; for a product or business, keep in mind that "a picture is worth a thousand words." An acquaintance of mine in the travel business recently launched a travel blog to attract customers and advertisers to her site. Entitled "The Artful

Passport," the blog features inspiring photographs from a variety of European destinations. Due to the elegant nature of the blog's title and images, you are whisked away on a journey the moment you start reading.

⇨ **Post an article that speaks to your audience:** As you craft your blog articles, consider the desired demographics, and be mindful of what you can offer your readers to spark interest and provoke a response. And make sure that you always use terminology familiar to your audience.

Six Benefits to Blogging

1. **It solves problems:** Clients, customers, and readers in general are always looking for new solutions or seeking practical ways to problem-solve. When you offer advice or helpful suggestions on your blog, people begin to see you as an expert. If your primary goal is to build business, demonstrate how your product or service solves a typical problem or improves a customer's situation. Achieving this will potentially draw increasing numbers of clients and customers to your blog and website.

2. **It builds community:** If you sell a product, blogging provides a unique means of connecting with your audience. When you post blog articles, you offer readers a chance to comment. And as you answer questions and offer suggestions, you establish yourself as the go-to authority on your topic. As your blog community evolves and grows, their comments can represent opinions from a broad range of backgrounds, providing a valuable opportunity to interact directly with a developing customer base. This vital give-and-take between you and your readers can mature into important online relationships.

3. **It drives traffic:** A successful blog consistently generates new readers and spreads fertile seeds that foster growth in your professional endeavors or the life of your business. This menu of options can help funnel traffic to your blog:

⇨ Share blog articles on your Twitter stream, LinkedIn, and other relevant social media.

⇨ Send email blasts of blog posts to current and potential customers, clients, or to related professional groups.

⇨ Send blog posts to LinkedIn groups or other online professional networks.

⇨ Include a link to your blog in your email signature.

⇨ Add a link to your website.

⇨ Guest post on another professional or business blog.

⇨ Be courageous and send a blog post to an influential leader in your industry.

4. **It provides valuable data:** A natural part of the blog experience is to share personal information. As readers discover and respond to your blog, they often bring up subjects regarding their interests, concerns, and need. They may also pose questions, or request your insight and suggestions. When you notice multitudes responding to a particular post, you can draw the conclusion that you hit upon a common problem or universal interest. Paying attention to such cues from your readers can guide you in exploring new content. This kind of reflective listening through writing will keep your readers engaged and attract others who share this popular interest. If you are blogging for your business, information that stimulates thought and conjures up inventive ideas can lead to generating new leads while retaining existing customers and clients.

5. **It maintains audience connection:** Sustaining the attention and interest of your audience is critical, and you can go a long way toward achieving this if you offer or suggest noteworthy possibilities. The key is to keep them connected by appealing to their needs. Include a clear call to action that makes it easy for readers to subscribe to your blog, ensuring that they receive all your blog articles as soon as they are posted. Everyone likes the word "free." So to nourish your readers you can offer free materials like

newsletters in addition to having customers or clients subscribe to your blog.

6. **It offers potential for recognition or discovery:** When you blog, you spread an inviting net. You might catch the eye of a potential employer impressed by one of your posts they happened to see on Twitter or LinkedIn. (The hope is that they will keep you in mind for future ventures.) If you are an entrepreneur, your blog posts might reel in partners or investors. And because of your expert experience and wisdom reflected in your blog, you may even capture the attention of journalists looking to interview you for newspaper or TV.

Blogging offers introverts a comfortable opportunity to be recognized for mastery in their field or business. And although your blog might not make you a star, some bloggers have been offered book deals based on blogs that contain noteworthy content and have developed strong followings. In the end, if you publish frequently and become a good online citizen by commenting on other people's blogs, you have achieved success.

LinkedIn, Twitter, and Facebook, Oh My!

Your head may spin like a whirling dervish attempting to work out which vehicle of social media will yield optimal results for your career development. Although you want to achieve the most from social media, the introvert in you may struggle with how much personal exposure is really necessary. With the ever-changing tides of technology, and the ebb and flow of the job market, online communication platforms continue to grow at breakneck speed. But you and your career cannot afford to be cowed by the impending specter of social media, and there's truly no reason to hold back. LinkedIn and Twitter will help you share ideas, experience, and skills with other talented professionals, whereas Facebook offers resources for today's job hunter as well.

It's easy to become overwhelmed when juggling more than one social media site. Downloadable applications like Tweetdeck and Sobees offer a dashboard that organizes your social media by keeping the posts from all the sites in one location. These applications allow you to create and send a message to LinkedIn, Facebook, and Twitter all at the same time. Dashboards can improve your social media life, and most are completely free.

Questions to Shape Your Strategy

Understanding your professional goals is essential to developing your social media strategy. So before you dive in online, ask yourself the following questions. Thinking about these questions in advance will help avoid confusion among the various social media platforms and focus your efforts in the direction you need most; once you've clarified your objectives, you can map out the most effective strategy to achieve them.

⇨ **What are your professional or business goals?** Are you looking to expand your network, seek partnerships, or promote your business? Or are you looking for a new position?

⇨ **Who is your target audience?** Are you trying to reach employers, colleagues, customers, or clients?

⇨ **What makes you an expert in your field?** Are you someone who possesses special skills and talents? How can social media platforms help you demonstrate these talents and increase your visibility?

⇨ **Who are the leaders in your field?** Would connecting with them on social media help you gain mastery in your career or build your business? Are you hoping to learn about new trends or innovation in your field from experts in your industry?

⇨ **How do you measure meeting your objectives?** By the number of readers/customers and the nature of their responses? Or obtaining new business leads? Perhaps getting contacted by recruiters or hiring managers for new opportunities?

Set Realistic Goals

Social media requires time and commitment, so give it a road test to see which sites offer the best route to your professional goals without eating up all your extra time. You may want to create a social media schedule, or use a chart to map out how frequently you read and send out posts, work on expanding your network, and read articles on current and future industry trends. A variety of free apps can help you design your social media schedule, such as Google Calendar, Basecamp, and Wunderlist.

As a final thought for this chapter, keep in mind that social media can be addictive. Maintaining an active presence on social media is important, but remember not to compromise a healthy work-life balance.

TALK TO STRANGERS

Whether on the phone or in person, striking up a conversation with a stranger often causes an introvert to freeze or offer only small bites of information. When faced with a classic extrovert, you may find the flood of information so overwhelming that you have difficulty finding a space to inject your own thoughts and ideas. Despite these challenges, networking can make or break a career in today's work world and rising gig economy. Recent surveys indicate that 70 to 80 percent of those seeking jobs find these positions—including new opportunities with their present employer—through an important connection. And a 2016 survey conducted by Lou Adler, author and CEO of The Adler Group, found that 85 percent of 3,000 participants acquired jobs directly through networking.[1]

You may be having an "Oh, no!" moment as you take in these startling statistics and realize you can't rise professionally without building the muscles of your network. But you can turn these deflating numbers into self-nourishing ones. Recognize that your natural tendency to listen, focus, and pose questions can further the conversation in a meaningful direction. These valuable and natural talents can make you a champion weightlifter in the arena of networking.

Furthermore, you can rely on your personal style to succeed in making inroads toward important professional connections. At times, you may have to move beyond your comfort zone and challenge yourself to stretch in new directions. But if you relax and let your positive inner force guide you, networking can be an enjoyable ride that leads you down the road of opportunity.

In this chapter, I share a variety of methods and a selection of tools to help you feel more comfortable as you address networking. By using this advice methodically and within the parameters of your own personality, you can capture the power of your introversion and envision a room full of people, not as strangers, but as potential allies and valuable professional connections.

Planned Happenstance

Several clients I've worked with find that John Krumboltz's Happenstance Learning Theory has supported their career development. The main concept is that you can transform curiosity into an opportunity for exploration and learning by taking initiative on chance events. Krumboltz believes that "luck is no accident," and if you are poised to take real action on keenly held interests, you maximize your chance of creating opportunities that will further your career. In other words, you can create your own career luck through planned happenstance, with a mindset of taking initiative and expecting the unexpected.

This "luck" is illustrated in Susannah's story when her initiative in networking turned into a surprise career opportunity. A successful executive for a real estate development company, Susannah was looking for new professional opportunities. She grew up in very poor circumstances and was the first in her family to attend college, an experience that totally transformed her life. Education and learning were high on Susannah's list of values, and she consequently succeeded in earning undergraduate and MBA degrees at Ivy League universities. Susannah's curiosity and passion for learning compelled her to transition out of the private sector and consider a fresh pallet of career opportunities in finance and operations in higher education. A close friend working at a local university gave Susannah the name of the school's vice president of finance and administration.

After a volley of emails, Susannah scheduled an informational network meeting with the vice president. She had no preconceived notions about the meeting, hoping merely to learn more about the VP's background and gain insight into the university department landscape. It turned out that the VP had only been at the university for eight months and was in the process of restructuring the department. In the course of their discussion, the VP's interest grew in Susannah's experience, skill set, and background. Finally, he suggested that she should work in his department. Not only was Susannah hired as an associate vice president, she was also able to negotiate and write her own job description. Susannah's curiosity led to action that stimulated a meeting and resulted in a desirable career opportunity. Even if the outcome of this meeting had turned out to be less favorable, the experience was formative. Who knows what other potential benefits may have come about as a result of this face-to-face contact with a pertinent professional?

Examine the Benefits of Networking

Networking can truly give you the magic wand that conjures professional opportunity. If you look at its powerful mojo, you can be convinced that it's in your best interest to surrender your reservations. Networking works best when you don't force it, so this chapter lays out specific steps you can take to conquer networking fears and support taking new risks. Then, use your gift of introversion to cultivate networking relationships with grace and your own personal style, and take advantage of the following benefits.

Opportunity

A simple conversation at a network event or meeting can be a lifeline to your future. When you take a deep breath and venture out into the open spaces of the professional world, you meet people at all career levels. Connecting with a former colleague or a senior leader could lead to a job opening or an idea that cultivates the seeds that bring your business to life.

A contact can also provide opportunities to expand your knowledge and expertise. I once attended a professional meeting at which a colleague introduced me to an author of a published career-related book. The author

(Tom) shared his experiences of the process and offered hints that became integral to this book's development. And I continue to stay in touch with Tom. A chance event benefitted me in the form of useful knowledge and a valuable, ongoing network connection.

When networking, don't dismiss unremarkable conversations as insignificant. An off-hand conversation with a new contact may open up the path to a business partnership or an energetic collaboration.

Visibility

As you open up to meeting new professionals, you share information about your work and exchange ideas about the industry's challenges as well as current and future trends. People sense your value to the field and what you have to offer. Your reputation has a chance to spread its wings, as people who matter learn of your experience, accomplishments, and skills. This exposure may result in you now seen as a go-to professional or even as an expert in your field.

If you happen to be a recent graduate or are reentering the workforce, no one expects you to be an expert. However, networking still offers you the chance to show off what you know and what you can offer a prospective employer.

Knowledge

As you meet new colleagues or senior leaders, you naturally talk about your work and professional interests, and express opinions about industry news and trends. During a conversation with a contact, you may learn about an innovative method or an approach you believe warrants further research or is one you might wish to implement at your organization.

Network Advantage

Many job openings such as contract work are not generally advertised—especially not in bright and blinking neon lights—so they remain hidden from view. Therefore, when you are looking for your dream job or you are ready to get ahead in your career, a network that casts a wide net can help you reach for the stars and land the new career destination you seek. Network contacts you have developed and cultivated can make introductions to the right people and keep you in the loop about other opportunities.

Picture the typical employer sitting at his or her desk peering over a stack of resumes for just one position. With all those personalities and accomplishments cluttering the view and screaming for attention, how will yours leap out of the pile to show what you have to offer? What makes the difference is word of mouth. If a colleague or senior-level manager who is a respected industry professional puts a good word in an employer's ear, you have a greater chance of being noticed. Praise regarding your work ethic and skills by a network connection who personally knows or even works with the employer can push open a door that seems locked and may lead to an interview.

Networking Events

These are the times when I admit to joining many of my fellow introverts and think of all the reasons to avoid attending a large venue. On the eve of a networking event, I find myself hoping that the event will be canceled. In the morning, I take a few deep breaths, put on professional attire, and push myself out the door, almost certain I am about to go over a cliff. However, I find myself relieved and pleasantly surprised by the time it concludes. Despite my introverted nature and predictable anxiety, the experience allows me to engage with others who inspire me.

Instead of the anticipated doom, I learn valuable information and lose myself in the experience. It's true you can network in different ways and avoid a large gathering, but there are times when breathing deeply and taking a risk can bring rewards and build a level of self-confidence that will take you to greater heights. Of course, do not expect to attend every possible network event; that would exhaust even the heartiest extrovert. Picking and choosing a few networking events per year can prove to be beneficial, while you bolster that strategy with one-on-one meetings and the appropriate use of social media.

Get Ready to Perform on Stage

When entering a large, noisy room filled wall-to-wall with people, all personality types can freeze up now and again. This is especially true for introverts.

However, even introverts can step into the limelight with confidence if they appreciate their own strengths and rely on what comes naturally. Tap into your reflective thinking skills to plan how to enter the room with a general outline of a script and some key lines prepared. This will ease your fear of starting a conversation and turn some of those strangers in the room into valuable professional connections.

Use Your Inquisitive Nature

Introverts like to dig deep when they meet new people. Often they tap into this ability by asking insightful questions that draw in the other person. Let your curiosity about professional interests inspire you to jot down the kind of questions that will display your insight, stimulate conversation, and form solid relationships. Writing things down fixes them more securely in your brain, making it less likely that your train of thought will go off track or freeze during a conversation.

Turn the camera's eye on yourself for a moment. Consider what truly matters to you and what you want to say. Think about which topics draw you out of your shell. Others will sense when you are speaking from truth and energy. Not only will you be more likely to offer a vibrant portrait of your experience and talents, but your energy will engage others and make for an animated conversation.

Your introverted self may start out gently, asking more questions than making personally revealing statements. But conversation is a two-way street, so it's important that you jump in at some point to share information about your professional experience. Keep in mind that, in this exchange, you may form a connection that can morph into a career-enhancing relationship. The following is a list of sample questions that will give you a head start.

Opening Network Questions

⇨ Have you been to these events before?

⇨ How long have you worked in this field?

⇨ How did you get started in your career?

After You Break the Ice

⇨ What keeps you excited about the field?

⇨ Which thought leaders do you follow on social media?

⇨ What do you like best about your work?

⇨ What major challenges do you face?

⇨ What trends are you seeing in the field?

⇨ Who can I help you meet? (If you have been to the organization's event before and know several people.)

Introduce Yourself

Given the two-way nature of conversation, there will come a point when you will need to respond or offer information. Although a fully memorized script can make you sound stilted, it's helpful to have some key points or phrases ready that you can build upon. Preparing these in advance will help you form and organize your thoughts to ensure a smoother execution at the point of introduction.

You might be tempted to introduce yourself in the most straightforward way possible, such as: "I am Sam Lido. I work as a software designer for SAP." Although there is nothing technically wrong with this introduction, you will probably spark more interest by opening with an explanation of what you do rather than your title, and then moving on to the ways you have added value to your organization. With this approach, you demonstrate that you embody much more than a title, and bring more value to the table than simply a list of responsibilities from your job description.

The information you might include breaks down into the Four Keys of introducing yourself:

⇨ What you do

⇨ How you add value

⇨ Specific interests or expertise

⇨ Position title and company

Let's look at how Maya, a personal coach, carefully thought through what she wanted to say in her introduction by using the Four Keys, then put all the points together in a short, two-sentence script.

⇨ **What you do:** I motivate people to live their best lives.

⇨ **How you add value:** I support clients in identifying what's meaningful in their lives and develop strategies for reaching their goals.

⇨ **Specific interests or expertise:** Work-life balance and how to deal with stress.

⇨ **Position title and company:** Coach at Dream Big.

Hi, I'm Maya. In my coaching practice, Dream Big, I specialize in work-life balance and stress management issues. I inspire people to live their best lives by helping them identify their purpose and create strategies for reaching their goals.

Launch Time

Even the brightest, most competent individual may have some trepidation entering a room that is already abuzz with animated conversation. If this is daunting for you, try arriving just as the event starts; this way you can initiate a conversation rather than trying to jump into one midstream.

I often take a few deep breaths outside before going into the event building, or I find a quiet space to consort with my brave warrior within before entering the scene. Create a sense of inner calm and well-being so you can glide gracefully into what might otherwise be an intimidating fray. Once you are in the room, make sure you start a conversation as soon as you can. Lingering too long on your own will make you feel self-conscious, and you'll only find it harder to break the ice.

If you notice a person standing alone, revealing their own hesitation as they survey the room, go over and speak to them. Chances are you will both be relieved and quickly discover you have something in common as you exchange introductions and move on to professional topics. However, don't expect every conversation to be energizing or mutually profitable. If things are not flowing well, politely excuse yourself, and rest assured that a better match is probably just a few steps away.

Build Rapport

A simple way to make a conversation work for you and build rapport is to use a technique called "pacing" based on neuro-linguistic programming (NLP), a communication theory that combines neurology, language, and programming. At the crux of pacing is consciously finding similarities that exist between you and your conversation partner. You might start by discussing basic topics like the weather or the environment of the meeting space. Then, as the conversation progresses, you can use pacing to match similar personal or professional interests. For example, your conversation partner might mention a new trend in the field that you are equally excited about. As you acknowledge your similar interest, you are validating your partner's interest. Or you might ask your conversation partner what they like to do outside of work and find out that you both saw the same movie recently, or that you share a passion for bike riding. Although the exchange of professional experience and knowledge is your main goal at a network event, you can enhance rapport by matching common outside interests, too. Note that this technique is effective for building rapport in both group situations (network events) and one-to-one meetings.

Make the Event Work for You

Remember: A networking event is not a marathon—you do not have to stay until the eleventh hour. It can help calm your nerves from the start knowing that you can leave once you feel you accomplished your mission.

Also keep in mind that you are not abandoning your goals if you need a short break. Go take a breather and walk outside or sit in a quiet room for a few minutes. Just experiment and find what works for you.

Wave Your Flag

Introverts are reluctant to put too many of their cards on the table when meeting someone for the first time. Your tendency is to be more inquisitive than informative. That approach is fine, but to build credibility and develop the depth needed to form a meaningful relationship, you have to reveal yourself just a bit. Perhaps share your genuine excitement about a project in which you are involved. Or without bragging, mention some accomplishments that might intrigue or impress the listener.

As an introvert, you probably find it easier to share ideas and knowledge than turn a bright light on yourself. But in the extroverted work world, it's your proven results that get the most nods. So as part of your preparation for a network event, have two achievements ready to intersperse into a conversation when it's relevant. This will further the conversation and place you in the spotlight. Avoid assuming that you don't measure up or that what you have accomplished so far is mundane. There are many achievements you can pull from your self-assessment chart or from your resume summary in Chapters 2 and 3.

Worried about boasting? There is a big difference between coming across as an egomaniac, such as "I am the best fundraiser in the universe," and simply promoting yourself, such as "I recently raised $300,000 for a new scholarship program by securing a grant from The William Foundation and from individual donations."

Follow Up

After the event, be sure to follow up with your new contacts. Here are a few ways to keep in touch with your connections moving forward.

⇨ **Exchange information:** At the event, exchange business cards and invite those who seem the most informative and responsive to connect with you on LinkedIn. Resist the temptation to simply use the LinkedIn prescribed note: "I'd like to join your LinkedIn network." Add a personal touch, such as: "It was so enjoyable meeting you at the AFTC networking event recently. I would like to stay in touch and continue our conversation on using Salesforce."

⇨ **Meet for lunch or coffee:** As a way to follow up with a new contact, create your own personal network event by inviting this person to meet for lunch or coffee. Use your introvert preference for one-on-one conversation to reach further into this person's background, experience, and knowledge. It is also an easy way for you to take initiative and cultivate a relationship that might prove beneficial to your career, either now or in the future.

⇨ **Power up your connections:** If you had a chance to speak with a leader in the field, don't be afraid to go that one step further by sending an email. This extra personal touch might provide the necessary glue to keep the connection in place. Here's an example of a suitable follow-up note:

I enjoyed meeting you last night and learning more about your career. Your approach to social media marketing is innovative, and I was impressed by your success increasing customers by 50 percent in just one year. I admire your enthusiasm and ingenuity and would like to stay in touch.

Igniting a spark this way can help you overcome the introvert's tendency to hide away. If you receive an enthusiastic response to your note, you might take another risk and invite this person to meet for lunch or coffee in the near future, as an opportunity to deepen the relationship and potentially receive valued career advice.

Most experienced leaders like to talk about themselves and what they have created and achieved. They enjoy giving advice and guiding professionals toward career advancement. Hey, it's worth a try—you might end up with a lifelong mentor or advisor.

⇨ **Form a group:** If you have attended more than one professional organization's network event, you have hopefully become acquainted with an array of colleagues. So why not form a small support group? I have been an active member of a Philadelphia professional association for career professionals, through which I have formed many rewarding relationships. I also organized a support group with four other career counseling professionals. To keep up with current trends in the field, we meet a few times a year to compare notes regarding our client experiences. The support and advice shared in this group is invaluable, and just knowing that I can contact a member with a question or concern is extremely reassuring.

Additional Networking Tips

⇨ **Volunteer:** Planners of large network events often seek out volunteers to help with the myriad of details, ranging from registration to setting up the event. Participating in this way provides an opportunity to get a low-intensity head start on meeting people before the actual event begins. You can alleviate your worries as you become oriented and familiar with the setting, meet some organization members, and establish yourself as someone willing to pitch in and help. In the same vein, you might volunteer with a committee for a professional association or work-targeted group. As you collaborate on special initiatives and projects, you will gain rare insight into their knowledge and skills, as well as gain a better understanding of your own talents and interests while developing strong collegial relationships.

⇨ **Set realistic expectations:** Be realistic about what you hope to get out of the network event. It's not about how many business cards you collect. You can still check off the experience as a success, even if all you did was engage in one lively, enjoyable, relevant conversation, or expanded your understanding of an industry issue by learning something new.

⇨ **Evaluate results:** Use your own personal Google Analytics to carefully assess the value of the event. Put aside personalities and sensitivities, and avoid being your own harshest critic. Look at the positive outcomes and be aware of what went right. Then assess one way that you might improve your approach the next time around. While measuring how things proceeded, keep in mind that networking is not all about you and how you sell yourself. It's also an opportunity for you to contribute to a professional community. Give your colleagues a chance to get to know you, and see how you can offer advice and knowledge, too.

One-to-One Network Meetings

Introverts are often apprehensive about reaching out to a network contact. Even if you have met the contact before, you may assume this person is too busy or important to take the time to speak with you. Or you battle the same lingering worry about what you are going to say at the meeting. But you can get over these self-defeating thoughts. Remember: Most people like to talk about themselves and enjoy sharing their experience, accomplishments, and expertise.

One-to-one conversations are an ideal means of learning more information and obtaining potentially career-soaring advice from experienced professionals. These contacts may become employment connections, clients, or future collaborative partners in the near future. And a network meeting will open the door to you on so many levels: You will become better informed about access to potential employers, the trajectory of industry trends, and the nature of employment opportunities within the field. Plus, it will help you prepare for the screening interviewing processes if you are seeking a new opportunity. Even better, it offers an opportunity to promote your professional background, skills, and value in an informal setting.

As with network events, the key to getting the most out of a network meeting is preparation. Focus on your purpose: What do you hope to learn from your contact? What do you want to share about your experience and career goals? What advice from your contact would provide insight on advancing your career or finding a new job? Once you have answered these basic questions, you are ready to move forward and reap the rewards of one-to-one networking.

Six Steps to Network Success

Research

Get out your magnifying glass and play detective by tracking down clues that offer insight into a contact's history, as well as career highlights that paint a picture of his or her professional path. It's easy to find evidence of someone's professional background and a quick summary of experience by reviewing your contact's LinkedIn profile. Use Google to discover any recent quotes or publications by this person. You might also check if your contact has received any honors or awards or is renowned for innovation in his or her field.

If you are meeting with a senior leader, you can search for a bio on the company website. Armed with knowledge about your contact's background and accolades, you will impress your contact as someone who does the homework. Take the time to research the person's company, as well. If you can speak knowledgeably and be up-to-date on services or products your contact partners with or employs, he or she will be more inclined to take an interest in you and be supportive of your goals.

Request a Meeting

Email a crisp and easily digested three or four paragraph note—certainly no longer than a page—explaining your reason for writing, how you made this contact, and briefly introduce yourself. Conclude the note with a request for a meeting, whether in person, by phone, or Skype. If you end up scheduling a time to meet your contact for lunch or coffee, be sure to pick up the tab.

Sample Meeting Request

Dear Nick,

I am writing to you at the suggestion of your colleague, Miranda Leto, who thought you might be a good person to speak to about opportunities in logistics and supply chain. After reading your LinkedIn profile, I am impressed by your diverse experience in the automotive, food service, grocery and beverage, high-tech, and health care industries. I would like to set up a convenient time to meet with you to learn more about your experience, industry insights, and any career advice you might have to offer.

I have an MBA from Indiana University. For the past two years, I have been working in an entry-level logistics position at Target where I assist in overseeing the storage, transportation, and delivery of goods. I have learned a great deal from working at a large corporation where I used my analytical and quantitative skills to improve storage rates by 50 percent. (Note: always highlight at least one achievement and some skills.)

My company has been reducing the workforce in the past year, so it's an ideal time to look for new opportunities and take the next step to advance my career.

I am confident I would benefit from your expertise and knowledge of logistics. I appreciate that you have a busy schedule but hope you can make time to meet with me at your convenience. You can reach me at this email address or cell: 222-333-5555.

Be patient. Your contact may be traveling or working on a complex and deadline-driven project. If you don't hear from them within two weeks, send a diplomatic follow-up note acknowledging the possibility of your contact's busy schedule and your desire to connect with them soon. Often a considerate second note triggers a response, but even if you never hear back from the person, don't get discouraged. Just move on to another network contact.

Ask Questions

Once your contact has agreed to meet with you and the time is scheduled, let your natural curiosity be the wellspring for questions that lead to a deeper understanding of the industry or company. Also let your interest generate questions that will nurture your own career goals.

This will remove the nagging anxiety of "Where do I start? or "What should I say?" There is nothing wrong with jotting down your questions and referring to them during the meeting. Your contact will likely be impressed with your thoughtful preparation.

After you shake hands and chip away with some icebreakers, your focus should shine directly on your contact. Choose some questions from the following list and make sure they relate to the contact's career history. After this personal beginning, you can move on to questions more relevant to gaining knowledge of the field and gathering advice about your career.

Sample Network Questions

Contact's Experience and Background

⇨ How did you decide to go into this field?

⇨ What do you like most and least about your work?

⇨ What are the major challenges of your job?

⇨ If your job were suddenly eliminated, what other type of work could you do?

⇨ How do you balance your work and personal life?

Specific Industry/Job

⇨ What experience and education is required in the field?

⇨ What are the most important skills to have?

⇨ What personal characteristics lead to success?

⇨ How would you describe a typical day at your job?

⇨ What do you see as the current trends in the field?

⇨ Can you work at home for part of the week? Do you have a flexible work schedule?

⇨ How long does the average employee stay at your organization?

⇨ Is this the kind of work that could turn into freelance/gig contracts?

⇨ When you interview a candidate, what are you really looking for?

Entrepreneur/Startup

⇨ How did the idea for your business come about?

⇨ What are your major challenges?

⇨ What have you learned from your failures?

⇨ How do you build a successful customer base?

⇨ How do you market your business?

⇨ What would you say are the top skills necessary for success as an entrepreneur?

⇨ What is your favorite part of being an entrepreneur?

⇨ What advice would you give someone who wants to work at a startup?

⇨ What advice would you give someone who wants to become an entrepreneur?

Take Center Stage

With attention spans decreasing and people of importance schedules more hectic than ever, the thirty-second elevator speech has become a popular means of self-promotion—a sales pitch essentially aimed at professional contacts or employers. However, elevators get stuck (and people really don't like to talk in them anyway), so I recommend the SAVVY formula I developed for presenting yourself to your network contact. This presentation could take anywhere from thirty seconds to one minute, but it covers the most important elements of your career and ways you have made significant contributions.

⇨ **S–Synopsis of your career and education:** Short overview of your career so far, and education, training, or certifications that support your qualifications.

⇨ **A–Accomplishments:** One or two achievements that you can pull from previous exercises.

⇨ **V–Value:** Specific skills and abilities that demonstrate how you can add value.

⇨ **V–Virtue:** Personal qualities such as "enthusiastic," "dedicated," and "creative."

⇨ **Y–Your interests:** What you are looking for in this field or industry.

You can read a more in-depth description about the SAVVY Formula, as well as experience a SAVVY Formula success story, on pages 98–100.

Close

When it's apparent that you have developed a good rapport, and the meeting has been sailing along smoothly but is ready for anchor, you might ask your contact if they can think of other pertinent industry people you should meet. Also, ask for suggestions on additional reading or other professional associations you might benefit from joining. And naturally, reinforce how beneficial the meeting was to you.

Follow Up

Write a short thank-you note expressing your enthusiasm about the meeting and your appreciation for your contact's time graciously spent. In the note, highlight a salient moment in which you learned something especially helpful. Doing this by email is certainly acceptable these days, but you can also consider the elegance of a handwritten expression of gratitude, as long as it is eminently readable.

Ellen and the SAVVY Formula

Here's the story of Ellen, a successful and bright social worker but a timid networker who used the SAVVY formula to transform into an effective and savvy networker.

Ellen had been looking for a new social work opportunity for two years with no luck. Her position providing counseling to a variety of clients in a mental health setting had its rewards, but as her employer increased her caseload, it became stressful. Ellen proved to be a high performer and well respected by her colleagues. She didn't understand why she was failing in the job search. After careful reflection of her interests and skills and researching other job options, Ellen decided it was time to transition into a more administrative position.

When I asked Ellen what strategies she was using in her job hunt, it turned out that her only approach was to send out resumes. Because this failed to deliver results, she believed she wasn't qualified and would never advance in her career. When I mentioned networking, her face dropped. Ellen felt she didn't have much of a network and regarded networking as pressuring someone to hire her. Yet, Ellen realized that she had a former colleague who was now a supervisor at Children's Hospital. She also remembered her professor from the University of Pennsylvania's social work program, who thought highly of Ellen's research and writing skills. I recommended she set up a time to speak to her. At the prospect of this very reasonable scenario, however, Ellen's admitted she had no idea how to conduct herself in a network meeting. Ellen and I worked together to devise a network script, using the SAVVY Formula as follows.

Ellen's SAVVY Formula

⇨ **Synopsis:** Licensed clinical social worker with MSW from University of Pennsylvania with more than fifteen years of experience counseling clients of diverse backgrounds and ages. *Areas of expertise*: marriage and family, parenting, eating disorders, anxiety and depression, and bereavement.

⇨ **Accomplishments:** Supervised and trained social work students from Temple, Rutgers, and University of Pennsylvania. Presented workshop on the stages of grief for 100 attendees at National Association of Social Workers annual convention in 2017.

⇨ **Value:** Skilled in managing cases, facilitating case evaluation meetings, writing and presenting reports, community outreach, and counseling clients using cognitive behavioral techniques. Leadership abilities.

⇨ **Virtue:** Compassionate, dedicated, decisive.

⇨ **Your interest:** Inspired by helping families and individuals grow and change. Acknowledged for ability to supervise graduate students and manage cases. Ready to expand leadership and advance to an administrative position.

Ellen easily pulled from this SAVVY formula to provide her network contact with a well-drawn self-portrait. It included major career points, elements that make her uniquely qualified, individualized skills, material ways that she adds value beyond the job description, a snippet of her personality, and an indicator as to her career interests. Below is Ellen's final product.

Ellen's SAVVY Script

I have been working in the field for more than fifteen years counseling diverse clients on marriage and family issues, eating disorders, anxiety, and depression. I have developed an expertise in bereavement counseling and recently presented a workshop to one hundred participants at the NASW annual conference. My director selected me to serve as the organization's official supervisor and trainer for MSW grad students from Penn, Rutgers, and Temple universities.

I am at a point in my career where I am ready to move into a more administrative role. I would like to combine my compassion and experience with my ability to manage cases and communicate with clients and staff at all levels into a leadership position. I am inspired by the potential for people to grow and change and want to help manage mental health organizations to develop and implement quality programs and resources.

Ellen's End Result

Ellen met with her former colleague Louise at Children's Hospital, and a few months later she learned about an opening there. The position was for a case manager who would oversee support services for children and families. Enthusiastic about this opportunity, she contacted Louise, who hand delivered Ellen's resume to the chair of the search committee.

Because she was already familiar with Ellen's background and talents based on what Ellen shared through her SAVVY script, Louise was able to bolster Ellen's candidacy for the position with meaningful, positive comments on her suitability. As a result, Ellen was scheduled for an interview and when asked to provide three references, she was able to include an influential reference from her former professor. In the end, Ellen was offered the case manager position. This is a compelling example of how network contacts can become powerful allies.

In your own case, you may not feel the need to write a full SAVVY script; however, you can still use the SAVVY formula as bullet points to highlight aspects of yourself that will guide your contact's attention, assist them in learning more about you, and ultimately better understand how they can be of help in furthering your career.

Long-Distance Networking

Don't ignore potentially stalwart network contacts and limit your possibilities simply because they may not live in your geographical area. It is a wide world, and if you stretch your horizons you will find that information and advice can often come from afar. Skype or FaceTime can easily minimize the distance between you and a contact, so be open to scheduling conversations way beyond your own backyard.

Phone Calls

Introverts tend to prefer the smooth conversational flow of interactions that are face-to-face and one-on-one. Lack of visual cues can make phone contact with strangers or those you don't know well feel awkward and uncomfortable. However, this is not an excuse for you to exclude long-distance networking. Preparing for a call in advance, just as you would do for an in-person meeting, can ease your discomfort and make the distant connection work for you.

There are distinct advantages to a network phone meeting you can use to your benefit. In place of those visual cues you rely upon, display all your props in front of you before you pick up the phone: your SAVVY script, questions to ask, and research notes related to the contact. Another advantage of phone meetings is that you can easily schedule a convenient time after hours for a contact who is too busy to talk during the workday.

Skype/FaceTime

The most basic preparation of all is to test your tools ahead of time. Ensure that technology will be your friend and not an irritating saboteur. Fully charge your cell phone, and make sure you are in a location with a strong connection. Put your computer through its paces to double check that you can hear and be heard during the networking session. If you will use Skype or FaceTime at home to facilitate the meeting, make sure your presentation is at its best by selecting a room with good lighting and an uncluttered background. Also, you are hopefully accustomed to that slight conversational delay or gap in time that often occurs, a frequent technical issue in the back and forth. Of course, *you* are part of the presentation, so do yourself justice and look presentable.

Find Contacts

As a keen observer, you understand the need to cultivate professional relationships to stay afloat on today's torrential professional waters. You might feel a little like Ellen who, despite finding a new social work position, thought she might sink with the small boat of limited contacts in her network. But don't despair. It's never too late to start searching for people to build your network.

Friends, Neighbors, and Relatives

People all around you know other people and can put you in contact with another professional. In no time those few can multiply into many helpful professional contacts. A few years ago I met a young man at a neighborhood party who had just moved onto the block. He mentioned that he had recently been laid off as a videographer and was looking for opportunities. As good fortune would have it, I was able to connect him with my friend Mark, who was a producer for a large film and video company. Soon after, I learned that my new neighbor had a substantive meeting with Mark, who shared invaluable information and provided solid resources.

Professional Associations

These associations further the development of their members' industry and educate the public. Many national associations have local chapters that sponsor speakers and create special events throughout the year. They provide an ideal way to connect with individuals in your field or, if you are in transition, learn about a new field of interest. Officers' and board members' contact information is often posted on the association website, so emailing an association leader can be a discreet way to find a new and potentially useful contact.

Alumni Networks

Many universities and colleges survey alumni who are willing and interested in providing career advice to students or alumni. Often this group of
field-tested people is organized into a directory one can easily access online.
These alums represent a vast array of fields and industries and can offer a
treasure trove of helpful career advice and support. Since you attended the
same college or university, you'll find that this is a perfect opportunity for
using the NLP pacing method to establish rapport; discovering that you
have things in common will be easy as a result of sharing the same alma
mater. You can tap into this rich network by contacting your alumni or
career service office.

LinkedIn

You can also gain significant leverage for your network by using LinkedIn.
Your first-degree connections have their own list of connections (called the
second degree), which you are able to view directly on their profiles. If you
notice a second-degree connection who you believe can offer information
about the industry or field you are targeting, you can simply ask your first-
degree contact for an introduction to that second-degree contact. LinkedIn
also allows you to join alumni groups established by most universities and
colleges.

Role-Play to Overcome Network
Performance Anxiety

If you continue to struggle with second thoughts about what people think
of you or the type of impression you make, role-playing with a trusted
friend, relative, or colleague may give you a clearer vision of yourself. Considering that even the most experienced actors rehearse and adjust their
performance, it's reasonable to think that practice could improve your networking interactions as well.

Have your role-play partner wait for you in another room. Enter that
room in a manner that communicates you are meeting for the first time.
Shake hands and introduce yourself using the script you created in this

chapter. Ease into the conversation with small talk or a question. Assess how the conversation is flowing: Does it seem natural, even considering this pretense? Then ask your partner for feedback on your posture and eye contact, and if the conversation feels smooth rather than stilted. Now ask your partner to expand the role-playing into three different scenarios.

Scenario 1

After introductions are complete, have your partner play the role of a non-stop talker. Then find a strategic spot or pause in the conversation to interject a comment about yourself. For example, "I experience the same challenges you do working with defensive clients."

Scenario 2

Have your partner continue in the role of the nonstop talker who chatters on and on, showing little interest in you. Find a diplomatic way to excuse yourself and move on, such as, "It was nice to meet you. I would like to have a chance to talk with some other members before the event ends."

Scenario 3

This time your partner will play the role of a quiet person who pauses a lot or responds only briefly to your comments. In this case you have the opportunity to draw out your fellow introvert using the strength of introversion you know so well. You might try to engage them with a remark such as, "Tell me what you enjoy most about your work."

Rather than feeling on the spot in this exercise, try to lose yourself in the role, and view this as an enjoyable way to develop your conversation skills.

Cogntitive Behavioral Therapy (CBT)

You don't need to be told that worrying is counterproductive. Imagine the worst, let dark clouds blur your vision of the future, and anxiety immediately builds. Picture an approaching cataclysm and you are all but inviting it into your life. In short, irrational beliefs, self-defeating ideations, and self-reproach over perceived flaws can fire up negative emotions and invariably affect your behavior. Although you can't accurately predict the future pros or cons, what you can control, to some degree, are your own thoughts.

CBT is a proven and reliable technique that can help put your negative thoughts about yourself into perspective, while promoting the positive thoughts you deserve. The basic concept of CBT is that our thoughts influence the way we feel. It seems that it's not external situations or events surrounding us that determine our feelings. Rather our feelings are influenced by our perceptions about the situation or event. So if you find yourself ruminating about an upcoming networking situation, filled with concerns such as, "What if I say something stupid?" or "I am afraid that no one will want to talk with me," you can argue against these thoughts with CBT strategies. First and foremost, confront your negativity by challenging your thoughts with questions, such as, "How realistic is it that I would say something stupid?" or "Is it really possible that not one person in the room would want to talk with me?" Then replace your negative thoughts with positive affirmations, such as, "I am approachable and intelligent," and "People are interested in talking to me."

This affirming self-hypnosis approach may sound simplistic, but to a certain extent, you are what you think. Think of thoughts as powerful construction machines that can either build or tear down the foundation of your self-image. Although it is dangerous to sink into self-destruction, it is empowering to envision yourself in a positive light. Denying your strengths and putting down your skills can become a dangerously negative habit over time. So as with all habits, rebuilding and retraining your thought processes will take time and practice.

Creative Visualization: The Power of Your Imagination

Creative visualization is an effective cognitive process that uses mental imagery to improve self-esteem and interpersonal communication. With your eyes closed, you can conjure up reinforcing images and scenarios that uplift and bolster your image of yourself. Let's say you have an approaching networking event or meeting, and the familiar anxiousness begins to creep in. To counteract your growing unease, try the following example of a quick creative visualization exercise (including both a one-to-one and group situation), or create your own script. Imagining these "pictures" unfolding before you can feel as if you are watching these positive results take place right now—an experience that can wield a powerful influence over your unconscious.

Creative Visualization Exercise

Envision yourself walking into the room bathed in confidence, with an expression that speaks to competence and poise. The room is not a familiar one, and neither are the people within it. You notice a person standing alone against a wall, and you approach him and offer your hand and a friendly smile. You brightly introduce yourself and break the ice with easy-going opening comments. You quickly learn that your conversation partner is familiar with your organization and knows one of your colleagues. The conversation flows naturally as you exchange information about each other, your work life, and knowledge about current industry trends. Expressing appreciation and a sense of good fortune that you had this opportunity to meet, you exchange business cards and agree to get together for lunch or coffee in the near future.

Fueled and reassured by this confidence-building experience, you continue your positive momentum by going over to a small group that is already engaged in animated conversation. Waiting for just the right moment, you introduce yourself. Showing genuine interest, you ask relevant questions and sprinkle in comments that further the topic already under discussion. You have an opportunity to mention a problem at your job and describe how you resolved it. One person in this group is a highly respected, senior-level professional who expresses interest in your approach to the problem and wants to talk with you further about your experience. You exchange contact information and move on to meet a few other professionals in the room. When you feel as if you are hitting the wall in terms of spirited energy, you make a graceful exit with the knowledge that you were successful and can add a new professional contact to your growing network.

Get Into the Spirit

Motivation often results from simply taking action. It's not a matter of getting fired up about attending a network event or warming up with jumping jacks to meet a new contact. Consider a time when you got yourself in a negative mindset and spent all your energy dreading an upcoming family gathering or work-related event. But then once you arrived and engaged in a lively conversation, you were pleasantly surprised by how much you were enjoying yourself and the company of others. This may have motivated you to initiate more conversations and scrap the early escape. The point is you don't need to be highly stoked or revved up to dive into networking. You just have to jump in and do it. With some preparation and simply imagining yourself sailing on that breeze, you may find that you get swept away in the spirit of things.

Take Center Stage: The Interview

It's a common myth that introverts are handicapped when it comes to interviewing. But this is simply not true. Comfortable behind the scenes and leaning toward quiet reflection, you demonstrate an ability to listen that draws people out and allows them to express themselves freely. These characteristics can work in your favor during an interview: You won't exhaust the interviewer with long-winded responses, and when the time is right, you are likely to come up with meaningful answers and insightful questions.

You may not be a glib small-talker who enjoys publicizing yourself on a billboard for all to see. You may also struggle to answer questions in full or shrink at the idea of promoting your admirable achievements and personal qualities. However, you can easily turn your uncertainty into a winning interview with some advanced planning and confidence-building techniques.

It is fairly common to experience some anxiety when putting yourself in the spotlight of the interview. No one is completely at ease when evaluated under this kind of social microscope. After all, a hiring manager and possibly a work team will give you the thumbs up or thumbs down, so it's normal to feel some nervousness about your ability to perform well.

Just keep in mind that no matter what the decision may be, it won't spell your demise. Let yourself go with the flow, and tell your professional story in a natural and engaging way—embrace your achievements and give the employer a glimpse into what makes you tick. The key is balancing your introverted strengths with a touch of borrowed, extroverted energy.

Introverts can fall short in the interview by not saying enough or panicking at a personal question. In this chapter, you'll find tips for interview preparation with specific guidance on how to select and emphasize examples of your projects and their outcomes—especially examples that demonstrate your solutions to problems and innovative ideas. In the pages ahead, we'll examine some real-life stories of introverts who learned to succeed in interviews using the methods described here.

Preparation: Lay the Groundwork

Let's first examine that critical period before the interview when it's time to prepare. This is the moment to review your own qualifications—the highlights of your experience and skills that make you shine—as well as how to describe yourself on a more personal level. At this time, you will also want to research the employer and, if possible, your interviewers. You will feel better prepared with a sense of the types of questions asked, so I will also examine three categories of questions often posed by interviewers, and how to use these to your advantage in telling your story. In addition, I'll discuss ways to practice your interviewing skills in advance—before it really counts.

What Are Employers Looking For?

On your personal radar screen, consider what the employer is seeking in an employee beyond obvious requirements like experience and qualifications. A survey conducted by Harris Poll on behalf of CareerBuilder with 2,138 hiring managers and human resource professionals across industries and company sizes examined what skills and qualities employers look for in job candidates. The survey found that 77 percent believe that soft skills (personality qualities and how employee relate and interact with others) are just as important as the hard skills.[1] These soft skills include having a strong work ethic, the ability to work well under pressure, and being an effective communicator, plus qualities like having a positive attitude and being dependable, self-motivated, team-oriented, confident, and flexible. Other employer surveys, including one conducted by LinkedIn in 2014, concluded that these same soft skills were equally desirable, but also highlight the importance of cultural fit, innovation, expressing your opinions, and taking initiative.[2]

You are not expected to transform into Superman or Wonder Woman and save the organization with super power skills. But you do need to come armed with accomplishments and examples of quality work that will reflect some of these mortal but impressive soft skills and technical talents.

Review Your Resume and LinkedIn Profile

A solid starting point as you prepare for an interview is to review the work you have already accomplished. Employers are likely to ask some questions based on reading your resume and LinkedIn profile, so anything you've listed on these is fair game. It's easy to forget specific details of a job you had five years ago, but this position may be of interest to the interviewer, so look over your resume closely. As your review it, pull out the projects and accomplishments that best match the job description.

The following questionnaire is designed to help you dig deeply into the wellspring of your experience and generate examples that demonstrate your competence and knowledge. These are also areas likely to be of interest to your interviewer. The payoff for completing this questionnaire is that you will be on your way to resolving the sixty-four-thousand-dollar question (not adjusted for inflation): "What do I say in an interview?"

⇨ **What are your major tasks and responsibilities in your current position and most recent past jobs?** If you are unemployed at the moment, use experiences from your most recent work. As a recent grad, you can pull from internships and leadership activities.

⇨ **What are your signature work accomplishments/results?** You have picked up from previous chapters that accomplishments reign supreme. List ones specific to your target employer, but don't leave out accomplishments that highlight your soft skills, too.

⇨ **What are some problems/obstacles you have faced in the workplace, and how did you resolve them?** This doesn't have to be a dramatic problem; examples might be customer complaints, delays that impact deadlines, technology issues, or a panel speaker not showing up.

⇨ **What skills and abilities have you developed and/or strengthened?** You can pull from a self-assessment chart or your resume, but consider any other specific skills that would be of interest to the employer. This is also a good place to list any courses or training that contributed to building your skill set.

⇨ **What have you learned about yourself through experience?** Think of defining moments in your career when you gained insight about yourself related to work.

⇨ **What excites you about your industry and field?** Reach inward for what you find compelling about your profession.

⇨ **What are some current and important trends that interest you?** Identify a few trends to bring up in your interview that demonstrate your knowledge of cutting-edge techniques or innovative ideas.

⇨ **What are some important decisions you have made at work and in your career?** These can include examples such as why you switched jobs or careers, a situation in which you reported unethical behavior, or one where you employed basic decision-making in selecting a database to collect information.

⇨ **How do you handle difficult people?** Think of some challenges you have faced in interactions with colleagues, supervisors, board members, or clients, and how a resolution was reached. If you are a recent college graduate, you can use professors or students as models.

⇨ **How do you work in groups or teams?** Think about typical roles you have adopted, such as leader, facilitator, mediator, organizer, and delegator, and how these roles have taken shape and evolved.

⇨ **How do you deal with adversity on the job?** These are bigger-picture issues than trivial workplace problems. Examples might be morale issues, major company or organization transitions, or reduction in salary or benefits.

A Sample Response: Alan the Librarian

Let's see how Alan, a librarian seeking advancement to a management position, successfully handled a typical interview question after reviewing his work history, skills, and education.

Which of your qualifications would make you successful in this position?

> *I began my career in library science by pursuing my graduate degree at Drexel University, one of the top Library Science programs. Since graduation, I have worked at the University of Maryland's business library at the circulation desk where I have had the opportunity to train library interns and initiate changes to circulation procedures. I continue to expand my knowledge by participating in professional conferences and taking technology courses offered at the University. I believe my project management and ability to build working relationships combined with my technology skills would make me a strong candidate for the Director of Circulation.*

Without skipping a beat, Alan fully answered this question because he took the time to carefully go over his background and accomplishments. With this self-portrait already in mind, Alan had a flashlight in hand to shine on his educational qualification, with two examples of success in his work (supervising interns and introducing needed workplace change) that reflected leadership, ability to achieve results, and willingness to share his knowledge with others. Additionally, he showed the prospective employer that he is engaged and committed to his field, noting professional development (conferences and technology courses). Because Alan had done his homework and examined the key building blocks of his career, it was smooth sailing when he was asked this traditional interview question.

Review What Makes You Tick

Now that you have broken down your experience into its various facets for quick and timely recall, it's time to turn to another important interview topic: what makes you tick. Think about what spurs you on versus what holds you back. It's inevitable that the interviewer will ask you questions that attempt to uncover who you really are, especially your more appealing personal qualities. For introverts, questions that seem more personal often present the greatest challenge. It's not that you are inept at talking about yourself, but your tendency is to keep your cards close to your chest.

However, you don't want to let a potential employer fill in your puzzle with mismatched pieces. Before being cast in the hot seat, take the time to list examples on the following questionnaire using both your head and your heart. Capturing your personal essence and having it at the right moment will help avoid any stuttering and stammering. There is a benefit to these questions: They often reveal your soft skills like work ethic, positive attitude, flexibility, and motivation. These are skills highly sought after in this age of hard, foot-to-the-floor acceleration.

⇨ **Describe yourself in three or more adjectives.** Pull from your assessment chart from Chapter 2, or list what naturally comes to mind.

⇨ **How would your colleagues and friends describe you?** Ask your friends or colleagues for some phrases or adjectives they might use to describe you.

⇨ **What motivates you in work and in your life?** Imagine times and circumstances in which you were captain of your ship and very much in the flow.

⇨ **How do you handle stress?** Think of positive ways you cope with stress, like certain exercises or support from positive-minded friends.

⇨ **Do you have a personal accomplishment of which you're especially proud?** Only list examples outside of work that you feel comfortable discussing. Accomplishments from running a marathon or reading a book a month, to helping an elderly relative or overcoming a personal challenge are all personal achievements. You do not need to win a Nobel Prize or be a triathlete to appeal to an employer.

⇨ **What are your strengths?** You can borrow some skill-based examples from your work experience questionnaire, but also focus on more personal qualities such as creative thinker, approachable, or sense of humor.

⇨ **What is one of your biggest weaknesses?** No one likes this question because you won't want to share anything potentially true about yourself that might startle your interviewer or throw you out of the competition. You might be a procrastinator, but you won't want to communicate that to a prospective employer. Select a weakness that's authentic but digestible to an employer, then focus on the fact that you have improved or are working on it. Avoid the clichés: "I am a perfectionist and a workaholic." Be honest about a weakness that's true to your character and wouldn't scare off your interviewer. Employers aren't trying to trick you. They just want to know that you are aware of your weakness and are taking steps to improve it.

⇨ **What are your future goals?** No one has a crystal ball or is capable of predicting the changing currents of modern-day economics. But try to form a vision of your career and how you might like it to unfold further down the road of life. Think of examples related to advancing to a higher position, skill development, and/or building competencies.

⇨ **How do you handle conflict?** Examples might include work project challenges or interpersonal conflicts presented by coworkers, supervisors, clients, or customers.

⇨ **What ideas or initiatives have you contributed to an organization?** Here you have an opportunity to display your creative thinking talents and conjure up examples that show where you have inaugurated ideas, designed effective techniques, or established well-orchestrated programs.

⇨ **What are your outside interests or hobbies?** There is so much more to a good employee than how they fit a strict job description. For example, an interviewer will sometimes ask about what you like to do in your free time, or to discuss the last book you read.

Andrea: A Sample Response

Andrea is a lawyer at a large firm who successfully balanced her introversion with the firm's extroverted demands. After a successful five-year run of legal contract work, she is applying for in-house counsel positions. As part of her job search strategy, Andrea wanted to polish up her interview skills. She felt confident answering questions about her education and work experience, but was anxious about the more personal questions, so we worked from some examples on her questionnaire. Andrea listed public speaking as an example of an area she wanted to improve. This helped her attack the dreaded question, "What is one of your weaknesses?" Because she had a chance to think about this question in advance, she was well prepared to answer it.

What is one of your biggest weaknesses?

I was never strong at public speaking, but over the past few years, I have taken the initiative at my firm to adopt leadership roles through committees, and to run meetings to help me feel more comfortable when addressing a group or the court. Recently, I was asked to present a seminar at the local bar association that was well received by the audience, even though I experienced some performance anxiety just before the presentation.

Rather than attempting to mask her flaw, Andrea came right out and emphasized ways she has approached her weakness that anyone would find reasonable and even admirable. Admitting that her challenge didn't simply disappear overnight, Andrea presents herself as someone who has the sense of self, courage, and mindfulness to grapple with a personal challenge and take action to seek out solutions that result in improvement.

Employer Research: It Pays to Be in the Know

While you are busy fretting over how you will answer the multitude of questions, don't fall short on fully researching the target employer. Enlist your introverted style of deep concentration and focus to uncover the nature and goals of the organization. What you learn from your research will help you articulate both why you are interested in the company and why it's a good fit for you. Your research will help you generate questions to ask your interviewer, as well as strategize answers to interview questions that demonstrate how you can contribute to the organization.

Inserting a fact that you learned during your company research into one of your answers will impress the interviewer with your knowledge and initiative. For example, you might be asked the typical interview question, "Why are you interested in our company?" The following answer effectively demonstrates that you took the time to carefully investigate the company.

> *I noted on your website that you are expanding your work in artificial intelligence (AI), and I discovered in my research that Computer World ranked your company as one the top innovators in the field. I want to play an integral role in a company that's on the cutting-edge of AI. With my technical, creative thinking, and problem-solving skills, I am confident that I can help build a promising future for Astrodynamics.*

Taking the initiative is a sought-after quality in today's fast-paced workplace, and this answer shows that the interviewee went the extra mile to gain unique knowledge about the company.

What You Should Know About an Employer

Products or Services

⇨ What are the products or services the company provides?

⇨ What is special or stands out about the company's area of expertise or product?

⇨ What is the mission or philosophy of the organization if it's a nonprofit?

⇨ How innovative is the company or organization?

Size and Growth

⇨ How many employees work for the company?

⇨ Has the company expanded or downsized in the past five years?

⇨ How many clients or customers does the company serve?

⇨ How many locations and divisions does the company have?

⇨ Does the company hire contract workers, and what percentage of total workforce do they represent?

⇨ Who is on the board of directors?

⇨ Will technology impact the future of the company, for better or worse?

Competition

⇨ Who are the company's competitors?

⇨ What is the reputation of the company?

Culture

⇨ What is the management structure?

⇨ What is the organization's philosophy on providing service or doing business?

⇨ What is the approach to work-life balance?

⇨ How many women and minorities are in leadership positions?

⇨ How does the company use social media?

Financial Health

⇨ What is the company's source of funding?

⇨ What are the company's assets and earnings?

⇨ Have profits been up or down in the last few years? (For a non-profit, look for answers in the annual report, current budget, and funding sources.)

⇨ Is the company or organization privately or publicly owned?

⇨ Depending on the industry, there may be other topics you want to explore further in your research, but this gives you a good place to start.

Fortunately, several online sources can help you answer many of these questions. The power of preparation will support your self-confidence and allow you to enter the interview well informed. If you can't find answers to certain points, this might trigger a thoughtful question to ask at your interview. Your interviewer will appreciate such an intelligent inquiry, which may stimulate a vigorous dialogue.

⇨ **Company website:** One of the best ways to get a feel for the organization's culture is to read through the company website. Is the website design and presentation appealing and user friendly? Are the organization's services clearly stated and the nature of the products clearly explained? Foremost in your website research should be practical considerations, such as the company's financial health and how the organization stands up against competition. Get a feel for the marketing strength of the services and products. Look to see if the website includes a list of senior team members with bios to get a view of the people who run the show.

⇨ **Blogs:** Reading a company blog is a great way to get a feel for spirit and personality. If an organization's website contains a blog, check to see if its topics indicate that the company has its finger on the pulse of current events.

⇨ **Company reviews:** Glassdoor.com is a career site that offers, at no cost, anonymous employee reviews with comments that bring the company to life. If you are a recent graduate, Vault.com is an excellent resource that describes company character and fiscal health details. In addition to providing employee reviews, these sites offer information about the organization's size, salary, and benefits with recent posts, videos, and photos.

⇨ **Social media:** Check to see if the company capitalizes on social media sites to inform the public of what they have to offer. Are they keeping posts timely and up to date? Is the content attracting a healthy number of followers? The extent to which a company puts forth energy in these ways will demonstrate how serious it is about marketing campaigns.

⇨ **Google:** The mother of all search engines, Google can reveal the health and nature of the company. News might include an employee honored with an industry award, company recognition as a leader in the field, recent attention in the media, or coverage in a trade or industry publication. It is also possible to find company flaws or pitfalls related to legal or ethical issues. Whatever you discover, information is king, and you will feel more in control if you know both the good and the bad.

⇨ **Insiders:** In many ways, it's "who you know" that can support your research. If you are acquainted with someone inside the organization, strike up a conversation about their experiences to get real-time scoops on the inner workings of the company and a feel for employee morale and treatment. There is no better source for information about the informal operation of a company, its strong and weak points, and its approach to work-life balance than someone who is living the day-to-day workplace experience. If by chance this inside person happens to report to the same manager that you would, this individual can offer you the opportunity to get a feel for the manager's expectations and see the kind of direction and guidance you could expect from them. You can also get an idea of how this kind of supervision might mesh with your own work style—or, just as important, how it might not. The chance to establish an understanding of the manager's style and personality, and then determine their expectations of employees, can be invaluable as you prepare for the interview.

The Judge and Jury: Who Are Your Interviewers?

Once you are scheduled for an interview, human resources or the hiring manager will usually provide the names of your interviewers. One scenario might be a single interview with a direct supervisor. However, as of the writing of this book, the trend for interviews is to include a human resources staff member, a supervisor, two or three individual staff members, or even a group interview with an entire team. To develop a sense of who your interviewers really are, you can employ many of the same resources previously mentioned. Check LinkedIn to read profiles, Google to see if any of these employees have been quoted in the media or recognized for outstanding performance, and check Twitter to find out if they've posted articles or interesting tweets.

You may also find that you have things in common with one or more of the interviewers. Maybe you graduated from the same university or are fellow members of a professional association. And as the interview unfolds, look for opportunities to show the quality of your interest in the company, and the initiative you have taken to learn about it. Mention a relevant point you learned through Internet research or social media about an employee, the CEO, or a director.

Compose Your Answers: Use the Q&A to Tell Your Story

Once you complete your career history and employer research, you can turn your attention to preparing for the question and answer (Q&A) session. Keep in mind that you are in a competition. As in any competitive event, you need to warm up, practice, and prepare yourself both mentally and physically, to ensure you have the best chance to make it to the finish line and win the gold (in this case, the job).

One form of preparation is to compose answers to questions in the form of a story. The format should position you as the main character who is professional and competent, but at the same time eminently likeable and accessible. Your story needs to retain the attention of the interviewer and keep them engaged. Therefore, you need to fill your story with meaningful details and accomplishments that the interviewer finds compelling and significant.

Three Interview Question Categories

Forget about trying to predict the exact questions that might be thrown at you. Instead, you can familiarize yourself with the three main categories of questions; then, learn the mechanics of the techniques used to address them. This will help you feel prepared and confident during the interview, enabling the story of your career to progress.

Career Background and History Questions

Questions related to your job history, career goals, and educational background tend to be the ones answered most directly and fluently. These questions are also the easiest to prepare for. For example:

⇨ Why do you want this job?

⇨ What have you learned from your past jobs?

⇨ Why should we hire you?

⇨ Why did you go to law school?

Although these questions tend to be the most anticipated, you can lose points in the competitive world of interviewing by omitting information that is highly desired by the interviewer. To help my clients compose complete answers to these questions I developed the SMART formula:

⇨ **S–Situation:** Context or example of circumstance.

⇨ **M–Motivation:** Your goal in answering the question.

⇨ **A–Action:** What you did to make things happen.

⇨ **R–Results:** What the outcome was.

⇨ **T–Transformation:** What skills or knowledge contributed to making a change or outcome.

Eduardo: A Sample Response

Eduardo, an introverted IT senior manager, came to see me because he wasn't getting any traction from his interviews but didn't know why. He believed that he was able to answer any question presented to him, yet he continued to leave interviews with a strong suspicion that the interviewer didn't really understand the many ways in which Eduardo had excelled at his work. During a mock interview session, I asked Eduardo, "Why should I hire you?" His answer was:

I am a good problem-solver and I have substantial experience in IT and process solutions. In addition, I have led and managed teams. In my career, I have taken on many challenging projects and succeeded in making systems more efficient in organizations.

Although not a bad answer, it provides no evidence to demonstrate that Eduardo is adept at problem-solving or making processes more efficient. In our discussion, it became clear that Eduardo managed to sidestep some impressive achievements and admirable skills, as well as his insight into his industry. Using SMART, we broke down the components of his professional achievements so Eduardo could expand his answer in a way that cites with real-life specifics how much he has to offer.

⇨ **S–Situation:** Example of major project: Process solution.

⇨ **M–Motivation:** Show how problem was solved at work and relate it to prospective employer needs.

⇨ **A–Action:** Developed model to reduce cycle time. Supervised team of twenty.

⇨ **R–Results:** Improved the change control process, resulting in a cycle time reduction of more than 9,000 hours per year. Model adopted across the company.

⇨ **T–Transformation:** Technology expertise, problem-solving, and leadership resulted in transformation.

Here is Eduardo's improved answer after using SMART:

I have both the qualifications and experience that you need for this position, but it doesn't stop there. You mentioned that your company finds it challenging to stay on top of the fast pace of change in technology. In my last position, leading a team of twenty, I developed and implemented a model that improved the change control process, resulting in a cycle time reduction of over 9,000 hours per year. This model was adopted across the company. With my skill in problem solving and implementing process solutions, I can help your organization stay on the cutting edge.

Taking his cue from the job description, Eduardo read up on the company's key challenge with technology and addressed this as part of his motivation in answering the question. He further demonstrated his professional success and skills by highlighting a specific accomplishment and demonstrating how his knowledge and skills achieved a transformation.

Behavioral/Situational Questions

These questions tend to be the ones that cause jittery nerves. Asking you to reflect on past conflicts or challenges, the interviewer will generally start with "Tell me a time . . ." or "Give me an example . . ." Relax. The interviewer's aim is not to unnerve you or trip you up. The manner in which you describe the steps you took to resolve a dicey situation gives the interviewer a sense of your poise, calm, and thoughtfulness you might bring to work in the future. Examples of behavioral/situational questions might be:

⇨ Can you tell us about a time you failed at something?

⇨ Can you give me an example of a time you were creative in your work? What was exciting or challenging about it?

⇨ Can you give me an example of a time you had a conflict with a coworker?

If you are not prepared for this type of question, you might freeze up, but there's a technique for answering these, too. The STAR method is a system to help you respond to behavioral questions in an organized, thoughtful, and relaxed manner.

⇨ **S–Situation:** Background information that sets the scene.

⇨ **T–Task:** Your responsibility.

⇨ **A–Action:** What you actually did to accomplish the goal.

⇨ **R–Results:** The outcome. Did you solve a problem or create something new or innovative?

Leah: A Sample Response

Leah, a successful event planner, was ready to look for new opportunities, but she had the nagging feeling that she wasn't putting her best foot forward in interviews. She knew she had to present herself in the best light to strengthen her position as a contender in the competitive job market. But she was unsure of how to draw from her pool of experiences and organize her responses in a way that produced impact. When she expressed particular concern about answering behavioral questions, I walked her through the STAR method.

Leah works for a company that plans and executes organizational conferences and large events. This kind of work is full of opportunities for minor and major disasters alike, so I invited Leah to focus on some problem scenarios. She provided an example of a time when she attacked a problem and achieved a successful outcome, showing admirable personal and professional qualities, and proving that she could learn and grow from a challenging experience.

In this example, her boss placed her in charge of a major professional conference held in Charleston, South Carolina—her first experience at this level of responsibility. On the opening day of the conference, her first major obstacle arose when she received a frantic call from the organization's conference chair because the PowerPoint slide projector was not working and the keynote speaker was about to begin. Here is what we pulled from Leah's experience using the STAR method to help her present the problem and organize a cogent response to the typical behavioral question: "Can you give me an example of how you handled a difficult situation at work?"

⇨ **S–Situation:** Overseeing first major event at large conference in Charleston, South Carolina, when the client, the chair of the conference, called screaming that the PowerPoint slides were not working, and the keynote address was scheduled to start in fifteen minutes.

⇨ **T–Task:** To fulfill contract requirements, address the needs of her client, and ensure that the keynote address started on time.

⇨ **A–Action:** Remain calm, reassure the client (conference chair), and quickly locate the AV staff.

⇨ **R–Result:** AV responded quickly and fixed PowerPoint slides three minutes before keynote address. Chairman complimented Leah on her professional demeanor in a crisis situation. Leah learned from this experience. Next time, she would check in advance to ensure that AV is set up and working properly.

Here is Leah's improved answer using STAR:

I was looking forward to taking charge of my first large event for the GALA Company at the Marriott in Charleston, South Carolina. When I arrived the night before the conference, everything seemed to be in place. The morning of the event, I received a call from the chair of the conference, who was furious and screaming on the phone. I could barely follow what she was saying. I told her that I appreciated how upset she was but needed her to calm down so I could understand what the problem was. She explained that the PowerPoint slides weren't working and the keynote speech to open the conference was scheduled to start in fifteen minutes.

I assured her that I would take care of the situation immediately. I called the AV cell number and also raced to the hotel desk to make sure the problem was communicated at all levels. Two AV staff showed up in the conference room within five minutes and corrected the situation just in time, with only three minutes before the speech. I was complimented on solving the problem in a professional manner by the conference chair. I believe that my calm demeanor combined with my communication and problem-solving skills contributed to a happy ending. Since this experience, I always make sure that AV equipment is up and running about sixty minutes in advance of the program.

STAR provided an organized approach that allowed Leah to tell her story in a manner that was easily followed by an interviewer. Just as important, Leah's description of the crisis scenario demonstrated her praiseworthy skills and personal traits including persistence, ingenuity, composure, and what lessons she learned from this experience to pave the way to smoother scenarios in the future.

Viewpoint Questions

Designed to reveal more of your heart and soul, viewpoint questions help employers get to know who you are on a personal level. They often require you to express an opinion or convey your philosophy. Some examples of viewpoint questions might include:

⇨ What's the most important thing you learned in school?

⇨ What do you see as some major challenges in this industry?

⇨ What makes someone a good leader?

There is no specific formula for answering viewpoint questions; rather, think of your responses as if you were writing a short editorial. In preparation, consider some salient observations and important realities you have picked up while working in your field or industry in the recent years. Ask yourself what style of management has brought out your best—and be ready to articulate that. You might bring to mind milestone decisions that made a significant impact on the trajectory of your career. To begin grappling with these questions—and avoid feeling thrown by them—refresh your memory on the driving forces in your work. The fact is that many introverts do well with these questions because they require more inwardly directed, thoughtful responses.

The following is an example of a well-composed response to a typical viewpoint question: Who has impacted you the most in your career and how?

I was fortunate to have the opportunity to work with a supervisor who was compassionate, organized, and highly respected throughout the organization. She had high expectations of me and team members, employing a management style that was firm but supportive. She saw my potential and challenged me to voice my ideas and create new programs, always acknowledging my achievements and commending me to the division director. Her confidence in my abilities inspired me to take new risks, like expressing my opinions at large division meetings and collaborating with other divisions on program development. With her guidance and support, I created an innovative program that still exists and is now funded by a major corporation. Even though I left the organization several years ago, she still serves as an important mentor in my career.

This response ticks off boxes on multiple levels. It provides the interviewer insight into the candidate's philosophy of good leadership skills (high expectations/mentoring/team-building) and personal qualities (guidance, respect, support), as well as how this leadership style helped the candidate grow professionally (taking new risks and creating innovative programming).

Practice Makes Perfect

Now that you had the chance to take inventory of your career, education, and what makes you tick, it's time for the dress rehearsal. At this important moment, a key element to interview preparation is practicing your answers to a mix of questions. This doesn't require you to write down full responses or memorize exactly what you are going say. Rather, try to think in bullet points, identifying the main ideas to cover, along with supporting examples you want to provide, as you tell a rich and full story of your accomplishments and experiences.

Here is a list of interview questions for the purpose of practice. You can also visit Livecareer.com, which offers an extensive list of interview questions, including specific questions you might be asked within specific occupational fields, as well as sample answers. However, steer clear of adopting someone else's answer to a question. Although it's helpful to learn from the way others might approach a question, trust your own authentic voice to speak from your personal experience.

Practice Interview Questions

This chapter has already presented a range of typical interview questions, and the following list provides examples that are designed to showcase your skills. These questions and directives specifically address many of the qualities and skills sought by employers today.

General

⇨ Walk me through your resume.

⇨ Describe a job or task that has had the greatest impact on your career goals.

⇨ Which of your skills is specifically related to this position?

⇨ What have you learned from your previous experiences?

⇨ Which of your qualifications do you think would make you successful in this job?

⇨ What kinds of projects or responsibilities motivate you the most?

⇨ Tell me about your leadership experience.

⇨ Tell me about an interesting article you read.

⇨ What would you like me to know about you that is not included on your resume?

Behavioral

⇨ Describe an experience in which you demonstrated initiative.

⇨ Describe an example of when you showed creative thinking.

⇨ Tell me about an important goal you set for yourself and what steps you took to achieve it.

⇨ Give me an example of a time you had to take a risk.

⇨ Give me an example of a time you went the extra mile to get a project or task done.

⇨ Describe a difficult decision you made and your thought process leading to that point.

⇨ Describe to me an instance of a conflict between you and your supervisor or coworker and how you resolved it.

⇨ Tell me about a recent team effort or group project.

About the Organization

⇨ What can you tell us about our company?

⇨ What specifically made an impression on you when you reviewed our website?

⇨ What do you think of our organizational structure?

⇨ What criteria do you use to evaluate an organization where you wish to work?

Practice Techniques

Try Your Hand at Role-Play

Even carrying some baggage of introversion, I have been frequently surprised when I walk out of an interview with a feeling of success. When I was growing up, I acted in community and school theater productions. As an adult, I found that my experience of expressing myself through other characters helped me in interviews. It allowed me to see the theater in the occasion and take on the persona of a confident professional, which, of course, was an integral part of me all along.

Acting classes are not an essential ingredient in preparing for interviews and performing well in them, but as you practice questions, imagine yourself in the role of a successful professional. Even if it feels like you're faking it, leave your reserved identity outside the door, and practice entering the room as your confident self.

Along with going over practice questions on your own, find a trusted friend or colleague to act as your role-play supporter and conduct a mock interview. Having another person ask the questions will give you a reality check. Review your answers and ask for honest, objective feedback. Taken in the right way, objective feedback can be invaluable when you go in for the real interview.

Take Advantage of Technology

To help you practice, take advantage of the technology that we use in our daily routine. Some of it may seem mystifying at first, but the array of gadgets at our fingertips offer an excellent tool, particularly for introverts who work best when they have the time to take a deep breath and carefully process them on their own.

As you learn to practice questions using technology, you can apply trial and error to sharpen your skills. Remember: No one is evaluating you—except you. Eventually, as you become increasingly at ease, invite an astute friend or colleague to listen and observe your interviewing skills and have him or her offer creative criticism.

Start by recording your voice as you answer questions using your cell phone, tablet, or laptop. Take note of your tone of voice: Is it engaging or too edgy? Is the quality of the content relevant? Is the way you deliver that content concise or rambling? Overall, do you sound convincing and confident, or tentative and unsure?

Video will give the most unvarnished and honest reflection of your interviewing skills, as long as you view yourself with a critical—but not overly critical—eye. Better yet, enlist a friend or colleague to ask you questions and control the video for you.

In this self-critique process, it is important to be honest about one's flaws, but not to the point of tearing down self-confidence. Give equal time to the strong points you see by appreciating the ways you excel in answering questions.

There's an App for That

Naturally, as with any need in life today, there is an app for that. Developed by Career Confidential, JobInterview Q&A is an interactive app that asks you five basic interview questions to answer on video, and the app will give you feedback on the quality of your answer.

Assess Your Nonverbal Communication

A well-known research study conducted by Albert Mehrabian, professor emeritus at UCLA, found that 93 percent of our interpersonal communication is nonverbal, breaking down into 55 percent visual (body language and eye contact) and 38 percent vocal (pitch, speed, volume, tone of voice).[3] Only 7 percent of communication actually uses words. These percentages may seem unrealistic, but other studies reinforce the dominating role that nonverbal forms of communication play.

How you comport yourself in an interview speaks volumes. Your observations of watching yourself on video or feedback from a friend or colleague should include an assessment of your nonverbal communication in addition to content.

Is your posture upright and reflecting confidence, or are you slumped in the chair? Are your eyes appropriately focused on the interviewer in a way that shows interest but is not challenging? Or are they avoiding such positive contact? Do you tend to speak too fast? Do you hesitate before you respond, which creates awkward pauses? What are you doing with your hands? Are your gestures natural or a distraction? Body language, pace of delivery, and tone of voice can compromise your goal of convincing the employer that you are the best candidate.

Put It All Together

The mock video interview is a valuable learning tool that can help carve a path to a new opportunity. Maya, an entrepreneur who established a successful clothing line, was looking for a new way to employ her skill and experience within the traditional workplace, but her interviews were dead ends. The mock interview revealed that she suffered from the introvert's Achilles' heel: holding her cards too close to the vest while failing to promote her talents and accomplishments. Beyond the verbal content—or lack of it—the video brought to light distracting nonverbal communications that distracted the interviewer from focusing on Maya as a desirable candidate.

Maya applied for a marketing position at a sportswear company, so I posed the question, "How will your entrepreneurial experience be an asset to Action World Sportswear?" Note the improvement from her initial response to her final response.

Maya's Initial Answer

In building my successful clothing line, I had to develop a good understanding of market research and strategy in addition to overseeing finance and operations. I understand all the functions that are integral to marketing a product. I am also familiar with how clothing is made, the importance of fit, and current style trends.

Maya's Nonverbal Signals and Tone

We both noticed that Maya started almost every response with a self-doubting, uncertain "Um." From the outset, she was simply disempowering herself and leeching energy from whatever answer she was about to provide. Maya also saw that she was literally bracing herself by crossing one arm over the other, while supporting herself by holding tightly onto her elbow. We agreed that this was sending a closed off message of tension and insecurity. Consequently, Maya was failing to come across assertively or confidently based on her nonverbal communication alone.

Following the Mock Interview

We were able to pull out examples of Maya's marketing achievements that would provide a fuller picture of her skills and knowledge, as well as demonstrate how she would be an asset to the Action Sportswear Company. We also used SMART to map out a more complete answer. She practiced pausing silently for a few short seconds before she answered to avoid saying "Um." We addressed her body language issues, as well. Knowing what to do with one's hands is always a question, so I had her place them in a relaxed manner on her lap or to the side. Given this thorough preparation, Maya was able to expand her response in a way that showed her depth of knowledge, experience, and success as an entrepreneur.

Maya's Improved Answer

As my business grew, I developed knowledge and skills to manage all the major functions of a business, including marketing, sales, finance, and operations. I discovered that I excelled at marketing, from identifying my ideal customer through market research and creating successful marketing campaigns. I designed and executed a social media marketing campaign that increased sales by 50 percent within a year. Pinterest worked especially well in marketing my clothing line because of the image capabilities on this platform. The sales results provided the funding needed to expand my business.

You mentioned that you are designing a new line of swimwear. I understand all the functions that are integral to marketing a product. I am also familiar with how clothing is made, the importance of fit, and current style trends. I know the challenges you face launching a new product. I am confident that my experience along with my analytical and creative thinking skills would help make this launch a success.

Having responded to the question this time with greater conviction, combined with a nonverbal message of strength, Maya achieved her desired transition. She was hired as a marketing director for a well-known dress designer.

Get Psyched: Overcome Fears and Create Optimism

Of course, fear is a normal reaction to interviewing or delivering presentations. When you are fearful or anxious, the brain floods the body with adrenaline and other chemicals to help you either fight or avoid the situation. This often causes a variety of physical symptoms such as shaking or a queasy stomach. In most cases, however, there is no physical threat. Pay attention to the signals of fear your body is emitting, and you will have time to address them. As you learn to take greater control of your fear, you will discover it can also be your friend. The chemicals released supercharge your body and give you more energy. The following techniques can help you control fear and anxiety, so you can approach your interview in a more relaxed manner.

Exercise

Most people experience a sense of well-being from exercise due to chemicals, especially endorphins, released by your pituitary gland at the base of your brain. Endorphins make you feel exhilarated and content. If you enjoy low-intensity exercise such as walking, finding time to do that the night or morning before the interview will help release tension and keep your mind and spirit focused.

Meditation

Clinical studies have documented both physical and mental health benefits of deep breathing and meditation. Meditation can help you stay calm and alert during the interview.

The 4-7-8 breathing exercise is a simple and quick four-step process that can be done anywhere. If you feel edgy the night before your interview, or your heart beats quickly in anticipation just outside of the interview room, put this 4-7-8 exercise into practice. Inhale quietly through your nose slowly to the count of four; then, follow these steps:

1. Hold your breath for a count of seven.

2. Exhale completely through your mouth to a count of eight.

3. Repeat the cycle three more times for a total of four breaths.

Create Visualization

Chapter 5 introduced creative visualization. This simple but effective technique invites successful results by conjuring up positive, reinforcing images. Here is a visualization script that either you or a friend can record and play for a few days before your interview.

Close your eyes and take a few deep breaths. Imagine yourself entering the interview room, shoulders straight, head held high. You greet your interviewer(s) with a firm handshake and take your seat. Maintaining an alert posture, you make eye contact and listen intently as the interviewer provides a short overview of the organization and job description.

The interviewer asks the first question, "Tell me more about your experience." You make a respectful and thoughtful pause, avoiding any nervous gap, and answer in a calm, measured manner that is concise but fully developed. It includes important facts with a proud summary of your accomplishments. When the interviewer poses one of those tricky behavioral questions, you respond without hesitation. You move forward with the interview, almost like a dance, in a natural rhythm and pace with the interviewer.

When the Q&A session ends, the interviewer invites you to ask questions. What you say impresses the interviewer, as you make comments and ask questions that are relevant to the life of the company and show the organizational research you have performed. The interviewer concludes by indicating continued interest in your candidacy and giving you a clear idea as to when a final decision will be made. You make a gracious exit in the knowledge that, whatever the outcome, you have given your best.

Naturally you don't have the power to bend the outcome to your will. But the unconscious is a powerful entity, and when you communicate with it harmoniously, what you imagine can unfold in surprising and positive ways.

Power Posing

Amy Cuddy, a psychologist, Harvard Business School professor, and author of *Presence,* has studied how body language affects the mind. Simply put, how we hold ourselves physically is a reflection of our self-image. Cuddy recommends striking "The Performer" pose before you arrive at the interview by throwing your hands in the air in a triumphant V and widening your stance. Hold this pose for two minutes. You can pose in the restroom of the company building or at home just before you head out for the interview.[4]

These techniques are designed to create relaxation and focus energy positively. Choose whatever approach makes the most sense to you, understanding that the intention is to fortify your mind and spirit so you can be your personal best at this important moment in your life.

The First Hurdle: The Screening Interview

Many companies and organizations now arrange for a member of human resources to conduct a screening interview. In smaller organizations and businesses, this will be conducted by a staff person, director, or even the CEO. The format is either a phone interaction or, in some cases, a video lasting about thirty minutes, with questions focused on work experience and qualifications. The purpose is to assess how you come across on the phone (or video, as the case may be), and therefore determine whether you are a strong enough candidate to bring in for a more formal, in-person interview.

The Phone Screening

A phone interview is generally not a favorite scenario for introverts, who prefer meeting face to face, where you can zoom in on nonverbal cues.

However, despite what you may think, a phone interview can actually work in your favor. Remember that all your research and key information is right in front of you, ready at just the right moments. One golden phone interview rule: Follow your notes and not your fears.

Phone Interview Prep Tips

You won't pass "go" and collect the reward if you don't make a good impression on the phone. So to advance with flying colors, prepare for the phone screening with these basic tips.

- ⇨ Use a landline if possible to ensure the best reception.
- ⇨ Find a quiet room and make sure noisy pets, family, or other phone lines won't interrupt you.
- ⇨ Keep pen, paper, calendar, and a glass of water nearby.
- ⇨ Pull out the job description and your resume.
- ⇨ Have a list of related projects and accomplishments ready, and jot down any important points you want to make.
- ⇨ Prepare a short list of questions that demonstrate your knowledge about the organization and the job.

Tips to Land the In-Person Interview

Remember: This critical first round is your opportunity to pique your interviewers' interest. Using the following techniques will help you engage your interviewer and make them eager to learn more about you.

- ⇨ Consider standing up during the call to give you a sense of power and aid voice projection.
- ⇨ As the interviewer delivers their script, interject naturally with comments such as, "I understand," or "That's interesting," or "Very exciting!" This kind of reflective listening will signal that you are fully present and paying attention. This technique helps introverts who sometimes freeze up if they remain silent for too long.
- ⇨ To avoid rambling, limit answers to three minutes or less.

⇨ Use pacing techniques to bring up projects and other work-related examples that show your experiences match the company's needs mentioned by the interviewer.

⇨ In the natural flow of conversation, speak with enthusiasm about your work achievements and skills. Some nervousness is normal and can initially lead to short answers, but "yes" or "no" answers are never an option.

⇨ Close the interview with a simple, "Thanks for the opportunity to speak with you today," and follow up with an equally simple thank-you note.

The Video Screening

Some hiring professionals now use one-way video interviews to conduct screening calls. The benefit to the company is that this type of interview is completely automated. It doesn't require the presence of an interviewer at all. Questions are posed to you via online video, and your answers are recorded. A peculiarity of this format, which can seem awkward, is that you have no one to respond to your answers, so there's no opportunity for dialogue back and forth. Instead, your video responses are reviewed by human resources and/or the hiring manager, and a determination is then made as to whether you will move to the in-person interview.

This style of interviewing can be unnerving because you have no audience. But prepare in a similar way you would for the phone interview; then during the interview, remember to take a gentle breath in between answers to maintain appropriate pacing and keep your anxiety at bay.

The Main Event: The In-Person Interview

All the practice and preparation in the world won't lead to success if you don't walk into the interview with confidence and a positive outlook; you'll find this approach will serve you well. We've discussed strategies for handling fears, so eliminate any baggage (beyond your interview kit) and put on an optimistic mindset.

You may be an introvert, but you are not a turtle hiding in his shell when it counts. Now is the time to stand up and let employers see who you really are. Even if you feel a disaster approaching, there is often a way out. We'll examine some common situations introverts face and how to solve them.

Also, recognize that your introversion can be an asset in the interview, so don't look for crutches to support yourself. Optimize the finer introvert's qualities at the interview by using your sharp listening skills to generate thoughtful answers to questions. You easily pick up subtleties like facial expressions and body language from your interviewer, so use these nonverbal cues to observe their perception of your answers (that is, whether your responses are sufficiently meeting their expectations). Introversion is also a plus because you tend not to ramble or go off in wild directions when answering questions, a quality that is highly appreciated by an interviewer. Even if your presentation style is not full of panache and dynamic flair, your creative, thoughtful, and observant mind can impress an employer. These positive facets of your personality, combined with your ability to work well independently and collaboratively, are all coveted skills and personal qualities valued in the workplace today. So embrace your nature and let your natural attributes shine in the interview.

Avoid Catastrophies

Interview structure and styles can vary. Some interviewers have a list of questions they ask each candidate they meet, while others prefer a more open and conversational approach. Even with practice and preparation, there is always a chance for something unexpected to happen during the interview. However, "unexpected" does not have to spell "disaster." You can still stay serenely afloat and drift gently with the stream no matter how it detours and meanders. Look at the following scenarios and take note of how you can avoid an interview catastrophy.

⇨ **Speaking too quickly? Maintain pace and rhythm:** Even though introverts tend to think before they speak, you may tend to talk a bit too fast when thrown into a challenging situation. Look for early warning signs of nervousness during which you stumble over words and overcompensate by speeding up the tempo of your conversation. As soon as this begins, take a deep breath to slow your pace. Don't let pauses add to your anxiety, and avoid the temptation to jump in with comments that are simply filler. Pauses are a normal component of music and a natural process in talking. A break in conversation provides a constructive space for processing what has been exchanged and for refocusing the topic.

⇨ **Baffled by a question? Stall for time:** Don't lose your cool if you simply don't know the answer to a question during the interview. Let your body language and verbal response show that you are composed when asked what seems like a question in a foreign language. You may be able to take a stab at the answer if you think additional time will help. You can stall for time by asking the interviewer for clarification on the question. The interviewer may suggest which way to go, or invite you to consider different scenarios. In this process, you gain some time to collect your thoughts and form a cogent answer.

⇨ **Totally stumped? Just be honest:** Occasionally, you might get a question that comes completely out of the blue. If you are totally stumped by the question, it's best to be honest and respond with something like, "That's an interesting question, but to be completely candid, I can't give a response that would do it justice just at the moment." Any interviewer will sense if your answer is coming from out of left field. Your attempts to cover up a gap in knowledge will only embarrass you. And being straightforward may actually earn you respect. Naturally, you don't want to do this more than once in an interview, but if the general Q&A has been going swimmingly, one belly flop will not be fatal.

⇨ **Facing a stressful question? It's how you handle it that counts:** Some interviewers will ask what seems like a trick question or even challenge your answer. I once interviewed for a university position, which included lunch with three deans. From the moment I sat down, I was tested by questions on the value of career development in higher education. Instead of letting it turn into an intimidating experience, I gradually relaxed and treated it as a debate. I was so involved in the discussion that I never got to finish my lunch, but I did get the job.

Questions designed to put you on the spot are not meant to elicit a right or wrong response. Much more important than your answer is the way you field the question. You are being tested on whether you handle stressful situations with grace and clear thought, or whether you become unhinged.

Different Interview Formats

Not only can interview structure and style vary, but the format can differ as well. Understand that interviews are not restricted to short and intense Q&A sessions—an interview may be scheduled over lunch, stretch across an entire day, or even take place over real-time video. Each has its own challenges, so you'll want to be prepared for the situation at hand.

The Full-Day Interview

The emotional stamina and the mental work out of a marathon interview schedule can be trying for anyone, but particularly for an introvert accustomed to quiet time alone to process and reflect after social interactions. You can manage and be enlivened by the glare of the spotlight for reasonably short periods, but the need to be "on" for four to six hours continuously can deplete an introvert's energy. If you feel yourself wilting, find a strategic time to recharge. After you have survived about two hours of interviewing, ask to use the restroom before you move on to the next person on the interview schedule. Use this short break to keep your mind from spinning and to recharge the spirit. Take some slow deep breaths, and don't forget to strike that victory pose (or use any ritual that helps restore your energy).

The Lunch Interview

Prepare some small talk in advance if lunch is part of the interview schedule. This is one situation in which you won't be able to deflect much attention away from yourself. Although it is perfectly acceptable for you to ask questions, keep in mind the main point of this social exchange is for the interviewer or staff group to get to know you personally. In addition to work-related conversation, this is an opportunity to talk about interests or hobbies that give you fulfillment outside of work. These can spark curiosity and open the path to a very engaging and lively conversation with your interviewers. Along with displaying that there is more to you than meets the eye, and that you are a person of dimension, the conversation may bring out that you share something in common with one of the interviewers. A common connection can often boost your chances of getting the job.

The Video Interview

This style of interviewing is face to face by way of a camera. Prepare for the interview as if it is in person, but take the following extra steps as well.

⇨ Select a room in your house or office that's uncluttered and has a professional appearance.

⇨ Do a trial run and check all equipment, especially sound, well in advance of the interview.

⇨ Dress as if you were meeting the interviewer in person.

⇨ Watch out for tensional outlets, such as tapping a pen, shuffling papers, and clearing the throat. The microphone will not cancel out these distractions, but magnify them instead.

⇨ Don't get distracted by the appearance of your image on the screen; instead, make eye contact with the interviewer.

The Second Interview

Interviewing is a protracted journey these days. If you performed well during the first in-person or video interview, it's not always enough to secure the job. An employer may ask you to come in for a second interview and sometimes a third to meet more staff or ask you additional questions. The request for a second meeting is good news; it means you sold yourself well on the initial interview and are being taken seriously as a candidate. To prepare, you still want to do a normal review, but you should turn equal attention to what you learned during the first interview.

The second time around is a ripe opportunity to generate ideas and engage in more detailed conversation with the prospective employer. Use your reflective and creative introverted energy to suggest ways that could help the employer solve a problem, expand services, improve a website, or create novel marketing strategies. You will also want to plan questions that help you move a step forward in your understanding of the organization's vision and expectations of the job.

The Aftermath

The Recap

After the intense experience of the interview, you may need some quiet, solitary time. Avoid using this time to rewind, examine under a microscope, and overly critique every detail of what you did, what you said, and how you acted. You did your best, and it's time to let go of what you can't control, so give yourself a chance to detach and reenergize.

Later, spend some time recapping your interview performance. As you replay, begin with the parts of the interview that flowed well and made you feel optimistic. Assess your mistakes and identify how you can improve the next time around. Almost everyone has an interview horror story, so if it was a bad experience, see what you can learn from it and move on. Your life is a novel, and this is just one chapter.

The Thank-You Note

Before leaving the interview, request a business card from each of the participants. This ensures that you have the correct spelling of their names and titles for any further correspondence or contact. Send a short thank-you note soon after the interview, expressing appreciation for the interviewer's time, confirming your interest in the position, highlighting something you learned in the interview, and showing how your skills and background are an ideal match for the job. Send by email or, if you prefer to write a hard-copy letter or card, snail mail is a good option.

The Verdict

Since you prepared judiciously and gave your all, you deserve to know the final decision. Your interviewer may indicate an intention to make a final decision by the end of the week, but if you don't hear anything on the exact date given, avoid making assumptions of disaster. Interviewers are busy people with project deadlines and operational crises, and a delay in notifying you does not necessarily mean you didn't get the job. However, this is not the time to be a quiet and reserved introvert. A few days after the date you expected to hear something, send a brief email to the hiring manager or HR contact to inquire about the status of the position. You will not be viewed as a pest but an interested candidate. If the position has been offered to someone else, express appreciation for the opportunity to interview and your desire for them to keep you in mind for any future openings. As always, don't burn bridges that might lead to potential opportunities in the future.

GO FOR THE GOLD:
NAVIGATE A JOB OFFER

All your hard work and preparation finally pay off when you receive that long-anticipated call offering you a job.

Instead of experiencing an instant rush of adrenaline, introverts can be rendered speechless by a job offer and fail to negotiate the best terms. But there is no need to panic or accept a job offer immediately. Trust your natural tendency to pause and reflect. Take time to digest the offer, heading off any sense of urgency or pressure. Rely on your own logic to methodically research salary ranges and the menu of benefits while factoring in your priorities and personal goals. Don't give in to your fear and discomfort by settling and accepting whatever is offered to you. Shortchanging yourself can affect your future earning potential because many employers take into consideration your salary history when deciding how much they are willing to pay you. It is unlikely that you will lose the offer if you ask for what you genuinely deserve in a direct and polite manner. The greater risk is that you don't ask for what you are worth and discover in time that you are underpaid; in this case, you may find yourself working day after day, burdened by lingering feelings of resentment.

In this chapter, I provide introverts a method for evaluating a job offer and show how the negotiation process actually takes advantage of an introvert's innate and admirable tendency to think through issues with care and deliberation. To demonstrate what you can achieve, I'll lead you step-by-step through the case of a senior market research manager who conquered his fear and hesitation as he negotiated his salary and benefits with great success.

You Got the Job!

After waiting on pins and needles for three weeks, the phone rings and the voice on the other end says, "We were very impressed by your experience and the results you achieved in your career so far. We would like to offer you the senior urban planner position at Black and Rodriguez consulting firm." You listen intently as the HR representative articulates the initial details of the offer, including the salary information. You are told that you will receive an email later with the fleshed-out details of the offer, including benefits. However, resist the temptation to reply immediately with a resounding "Yes!" even though you are excited and eager to accept the offer. Instead, respond in a way that reinforces your enthusiasm for the position and lets them know that you look forward to reviewing the offer:

> *This is terrific news, and I am very excited about working for Black and Rodriguez. I look forward to your email so I can review the offer, including the benefits package. I will contact you if I have any questions. When do you need to hear back from me?*

This signals that you are considering negotiating terms and want to carefully review the offer, with an opportunity to contact HR with questions, before giving your reply. Most employers will allow you three to five days to review an offer before you engage in any negotiations.

Money Isn't Everything

Before you get down to brass tacks of evaluating a job offer, consider the various ways this opportunity will support and advance your career. What potential does this job have for strengthening your skills, increasing your knowledge, and growing your network? Often, the major attraction in pursuing a fresh opportunity is the fact that it presents a challenge, even if it may be intimidating at first glance. Taking risks often tests the comfort level of the most secure individual. But you take a bigger gamble by missing out on an opportunity to nourish and progress in your career; for example, even if an offer is "only" a lateral move, it may present a different kind of experience with opportunities to bolster your professional skills.

Note: If you are a recent graduate or reentering the workforce, it may be difficult to negotiate for a higher salary, because you can't use professional experience as leverage. However, if you have acquired specialized knowledge or technical skills that are in high demand to the employer, you may have some bargaining power. Either way, pay attention to the techniques covered in this chapter. These are not just useful in the short term; as you forge ahead, these techniques will prove valuable throughout the development of your career.

First Things First: Consider Your Current Stats

To take full advantage of the negotiating process, first assess your current or most recent salary and benefit package. Often, the focus of your angst in negotiation regards salary. But in concentrating on salary, don't lose sight of your benefits, as these also convert into money. If your current employer is paying your full health benefits, it may be no gain at all—or even a loss—if the new employer increases your salary but only covers 50 percent of your health insurance.

Have the breakdown of your current salary and benefits right in front of you before the written offer ever comes in. When you receive the full offer in writing, you can make an intelligent and informed comparison between your current salary and benefits and what's laid out in the job offer. Even if you end up not accepting this offer, you can take all the work you have done to break down your existing salary and benefits and apply it to another offer down the road.

Your Recent Salary and Benefit Chart

The following chart is designed to help assess and quantify your most recent benefit package. Pay special attention to health insurance. Depending on your age and health status, you could be looking at a difference in cost between $5,000 to $10,000 between your current plan and the new employer's health insurance coverage presented in your job offer. If you are a gig worker, you might not have the kind of generous benefits offered to permanent employees, but don't let that stop you from carefully evaluating your needs and current salary range.

View this process as a short research project that uses your introverted energy to clearly identify the specifics of your salary and benefits. Once you calculate your most recent benefit and salary history, you will be in a powerful position because you'll be armed with real numbers.

Current Salary and Benefit Chart

	Current Job	New Job
Amount		
Salary		
Bonus		
Commission		
Profit Sharing		
Benefits		
Health Insurance		
Employer Contribution		
Your Contribution (include copays)		
Dental/Vision		
Employer Contribution		

Your Contribution		
Time Off		
Vacation Days		
Sick Days		
Professional Development (conferences/training)		
Tuition Remission		
Retirement		
Employer Contribution		
Your Contribution		
Disability		
Life Insurance		
Expense Account (gas, travel, etc.)		
Computer/Phone		
Flextime		
Additional		

Let the Negotiations Begin

Once you have plugged in the numbers related to your salary and benefit history, you can take the lead in a fact-based conversation with the hiring manager regarding your job offer. It is normal to feel some stress anticipating the need to negotiate certain terms of the offer, but don't let the timid side of your introverted nature creep in and take control. Decide that using the strengths of introversion will further rather than frustrate your efforts as you stride toward a successful negotiation.

Believe in Yourself

Before involving yourself with the details of salary and benefits, you need to understand your own worth. Introverts tend to be modest and avoid boasting, but this is not the time to swim against the tide. Instead, review your proud history of achievements, and then let your skill set shine. Remind yourself of the quality and extent of your experience, and take note of your industry knowledge or expertise. Then stack all of the hard-earned work and accomplishments up against the needs and requirements of the job description; this will demonstrate to the employer the numerous assets you bring to the table that will make you a valued member of the team.

It is okay to feel lucky that you received this offer, but balance that moment of appreciation with self-appreciation, and realize that the employer is just as lucky to have you join their organization.

Perform a Salary Analysis

After you receive the offer, the most obvious and basic area for careful analysis is salary. Some excellent online resources are available to help you research and evaluate salary ranges specifically related to your potential position. Payscale offers a free online survey that invites you to plug in the expected position title, years of experience in the field or industry, and the city where the position is located. You will also be asked for current or most recent compensation (which you already have from the salary/benefit chart). Once you complete the Payscale survey, you will receive a salary range for your expected position. You can check out additional online salary survey resources, such as Salarywizard, Salary.com, and LinkedIn Salary.

If you are a recent graduate, go to the National Association of Colleges and Employers' (NACE) online annual salary survey. Check out the NACE Salary Calculator Center for the most accurate salary data on college graduates. You might also contact your alma mater's career service office and ask for recent graduate placement surveys. Here you will find a listing of salaries for a range of positions secured by alumni at a variety of companies.

Other factors, such as company size and location, may impact compensation ranges. For example, early-stage startups may not pay as much as businesses with an established history. However, working for a startup is an opportunity to take on an assortment of roles, as opposed to working for a more traditional establishment in which one can get pigeonholed into just a single function. If the startup is successful, you might also benefit from stock options. This type of blooming and energizing work environment could be worth whatever salary you might trade it for and provide you with a diverse set of skills.

Once the official job offer arrives, you can plug in the numbers using the same chart you employed for your current compensation. This will give you a clear comparison of salary against benefits.

Should You Negotiate Salary?

You might be surprised to learn that most employers are not locked into the salary they initially quote; rather, they expect that you will negotiate. The typical large business or corporation generally has wiggle room in a range of $5,000 to $10,000. For a higher-level executive position, this range may be more liberal. For nonprofits, the range of motion is more subtle, closer to the $2,500 to $5,000 range, unless an executive-level position is in the offing.

Don't let your status as a recent college graduate cause you to undercut yourself. You may still have some power to negotiate to the tune of $500 to $1,000 based on past experiences and achievements in the field through internships, leadership, or volunteer activities.

The greatest saboteur in salary negotiations is self-doubt. Don't let your angst or fears rob you of a lifetime of hard-earned income. Ask for more because you have done your homework, understand your worth, and know you deserve it.

A recent study conducted by researchers at George Mason University and Temple University found that individuals who negotiated salaries compared with those who didn't negotiate increased their starting pay by an average of $5,000.[1] Therefore, if you have researched salary ranges for your position and analyzed your value, and you still believe you deserve a higher starting salary, be courageous and ask for it.

Investigate Options for Benefits

Salary may be the first element that comes to mind, but it is only one side of the negotiating coin. Place equal consideration on the benefits package. Larger companies will probably have a menu of benefits and policies related to health insurance, leave, and disability arrangements. If these are written in stone, you may not have quite as much leverage to cobble together a custom-made benefits package. Therefore, be aware of additional options the employer may be open to discussing; these usually don't involve a monetary investment by the company but may connect with your deeply held career vision or long-term ambitions. Although it's normal to want to further your income, don't minimize the goal of furthering happiness in your life, too. Here are some possibilities to consider for negotiations that focus more on personal career goals.

⇨ **Position title:** You are excited about assuming more responsibility in this new position, but you feel the job title doesn't accurately reflect your promotion to a higher level or scope of responsibility. Job titles can vary depending on the size of the organization and company culture; to research various job titles with similar responsibilities, you can use the same online salary surveys already discussed. You might also speak with colleagues to identify trends in titles that match your job description and operational experience.

If you've done your research and you are still dissatisfied with the title presented in the offer, suggest one you believe better reflects your career advancement and scope of responsibility in this new position. Career advancement can be affected by something as simple as a title, so keep in mind that your trip up the future ladder is what you are negotiating here—and it won't cost the company a penny!

⇨ **Time off:** Enriching your personal life can make the compensation package more desirable, too. Although work life is at the forefront of your thinking at this crucial time, the fact that you have a life beyond work may be worth considering as a point for negotiation. A few extra paid days off can be a welcome boost to your compensation package and balance your personal life at the same time. And this, too, won't injure the company's bottom line.

⇨ **Flextime:** According to a national study conducted by the Families and Work Institute, Society for Human Resource Management, and When Work Works organizations in 2013, the majority of companies offer a flextime option to some of its employees.[2] This takes the form of flexible work schedules, working part of the week at home, or telecommuting. Several other research studies found that where this kind of flexibility is available, workers were more productive and less likely to leave their jobs. Introverts are often attracted to this type of benefit since it appeals to their need for a break in the action. They enjoy the tranquility and solo time to perform work tasks at home or perched in a quiet corner at Starbucks. Before tossing the flextime card onto the table, however, be sure to determine existing company policy and history.

⇨ **Professional development:** In this age of acceleration, you are expected to continuously increase your knowledge base and sharpen your skills. If you hit a wall regarding salary, you might negotiate for reimbursement for learning experiences such as tuition, leadership training, professional association membership, or conference fees. These are not benefits that threaten to bust a company's budget and will demonstrate that you have high ambitions and will bring learning and professionalism into the workplace. Also, these professional development experiences provide you with the opportunity to expand your network and professional visibility. Better yet, such opportunities for professional development can advance your career in the future.

Explore Compensation Packages

Once you complete the salary research and carefully review the total compensation offered, identify what an ideal compensation package would look like to you. First off, this package should recognize and respect your market value. Start by determining the highest possible salary and benefits combination you would like to receive and the lowest you would be willing to accept. Failing to think through the highest and lowest acceptable figures will put you in a position of hesitation. This could result in gumming up the flow of the negotiation and threaten your chance of negotiating a compensation package that you can live with. Having your aspirational high and acceptable low in mind can potentially result in a final offer somewhere in the middle, giving you better terms than you started with. Let's see how Carol, a young physician, negotiated an offer to work at a larger practice once she took the time to evaluate her priorities and research salary ranges.

Negotiation for Salary and Specific Needs: Carol the Physician

Carol, a family practice physician with four years of experience, makes an annual salary of $130,000 with full health benefits and a 401(k) retirement plan. She was offered a great opportunity to work at a larger practice with a salary of $140,000 and similar benefits. She is a single parent of a five-year-old son, and although she understands the demands of family practice, she wants to make sure she has quality time to spend with her young child. She has also been approached to teach a course on patient care at the medical school nearby—a career opportunity she looks forward to accepting.

Carol discovered that in her area, the average salary of family practice physicians with more than five years' experience is $158,000. After analyzing the package offered by the employer, she wants her annual salary to be closer to $150,000 because it's a larger practice that will require some advanced responsibilities. She would also like to negotiate a flexible work schedule so she can spend time with her son and teach the patient care course, too. Based on her experience and skill set, she is not comfortable accepting a salary under $145,000 unless there is some give and take on benefits.

In the negotiations, she promoted her achievements and knowledge in family medicine to convince the partners of her worth and to consider offering her a higher salary and a flexible work schedule. She also used her research on salary ranges as a key point in the negotiations, which ultimately helped turn the outcome in her favor.

As a counter-offer, Carol was offered a salary of $148,000 with a flexible work schedule during which she can work 7 a.m. to 3 p.m. four days a week and then have the day off on Mondays. Because Carol had opened negotiations with a clear idea of highest and lowest salary and her top benefit option, she ended up with more; ultimately, she secured a salary on the higher end of her range, and a flexible working schedule that allows her quality time with her son and the opportunity to teach a course at the medical school.

Have a Strategy

Approach the negotiation process with the same preparation you would give to any important presentation. Treat it as a formal conversation for which you come prepared with organized thoughts and have practiced your delivery to the point that you sound fluent rather than stilted. Remember: This is not a competition. It is about establishing a meaningful relationship by listening earnestly, speaking up, and communicating clearly and effectively. Imagine that you and your hiring manager are allies, working together to solve a common problem. The viewpoint of each party is respectfully considered, each has the opportunity to voice their concern, and a final decision is reached that is mutually agreeable and satisfying. As an introvert you are expert at drawing out and processing the needs of the others, but make sure that the outcome of the dialogue is truly mutual and not a one-sided affair at your expense.

Six Points to Developing Your Strategy

As you define your goals, keep in mind that the big picture can be seen from two different perspectives: the employer's needs and your personal career goals. To help you think strategically, consider the following six points:

1. **You want the job:** Be clear from the start of the conversation with an HR or hiring manager that you are genuinely excited and serious about the job offer. From this point of view, you have every right to negotiate for the best possible package. As you proceed, reinforce that your overriding interest and intention is to be the best match for the employer.

2. **They want you:** The employer is your ally now. Consider that, out of the multitude of resumes reviewed, and out of all the other candidates interviewed for the position, you made the final cut. The already existing good feelings for you will be reinforced if you present your terms politely and diplomatically. When nervousness

creeps up, recall the fact that the terms you request will allow you to be a more effective and harmonious employee. Keep in mind that you can be firm and persistent without being demanding or obnoxious.

3. **Make sure they understand your value:** Your most powerful bargaining chip is your own flesh-and-blood market value. Don't let your anticipation or nervousness about what you are going to say in the negotiations offset the worth of what you bring to the table. Shift your thoughts to the positive qualities that secured your job offer in the first place: the record of your job performance, your hard-won achievements, and the array of your proven talents and skills. Add to this your research on salary ranges and benefits, and you have a convincing case for advocating for higher salary and better benefits.

4. **How badly do they need you?** If there is a current demand in the job market for your experience, skills, and expertise, you may have a powerful bargaining chip to negotiate a better compensation package. Also, if there is an urgency to fill the position, the hiring manager may feel pressure to hire someone quickly. Whereas you don't necessarily want to take advantage of the employer's position, there is nothing immoral about benefiting from good timing while seizing upon a position of strength. This is the optimal result of negotiations when both parties profit: the company obtains the services they need in a timely fashion, and you will be a happy employee who looks forward to coming to work every day.

5. **Understand whom you are bargaining with:** Knowing something about the personality, position, and needs of the person you are negotiating with can be valuable and provide leverage that may ease the process. At some point in the interview process, for example, the hiring manager may have expressed concern about the nature of your position. Or perhaps they hinted at organizational trends or challenges that might impact your position and division. Based on these issues, you might offer cogent suggestions or confidently point out how your specific strengths will be an

asset in attacking problems and ameliorating concerns in the current organizational climate.

The nature of negotiations may also vary depending on whether you are dealing directly with the boss or with the HR representative. The boss may have the power to approve a more attractive salary request. It makes sense that they are more invested in advocating for you because they will directly benefit from bringing you on board. An HR professional may feel the need to adhere to fixed salary caps and benefit offerings.

6. **Gauge your bargaining position:** You may have a stronger position in negotiating a job offer if you are currently employed than if you are out of work. Similarly, you may pull more weight if you received additional job offers. However, be careful not to pit organizations against each other, or you could lose them all.

Prepare a Negotiation Plan

As an introvert you naturally lean toward focused and methodical thinking. These are characteristics that lend themselves to creating a good strategy for negotiations. Once you have time to process and think through your approach, write down your priorities and goals, drafting a script or bulleted list of negotiation terms that will help you come to an agreement. Similar to interviewing, practicing out loud with a friend or colleague can also help you fix salient points in your mind and develop a polished presentation (when rehearsing, use the following outline for negotiation presentation as a guide). This kind of rehearsing can also reveal whether you are persuasive in your arguments. "Practice makes perfect," as they say, and it will certainly make you feel more prepared and confident once you start the negotiation process.

Negotiation Presentation Outline

⇨ **Confirmation:** Reinforcing your interest in the position from the start.

⇨ **Salary analysis:** Presenting your research and salary analysis, and stating the reasons for requesting a higher salary (if this is a term you want to negotiate).

⇨ **Benefit review:** Review of benefit package and points for negotiation of benefits.

⇨ **Priorities:** Desired highest and lowest salary or benefits you will accept.

⇨ **Personal market value:** What you personally bring to the table: your experience, achievements, and skills that support the employer's needs.

⇨ **Appreciation:** Expressing gratitude for the employer's consideration of your request.

Adam: Negotiating a Job Offer

Adam, a quiet and successful senior market research manager in Baltimore was offered a position as vice president of market research for a digital technology company in Boston. He was genuinely excited about the company and a position that would advance his career, but he clammed up when I approached him about evaluating and negotiating the offer. Since the offer already constituted a promotion with a higher salary, Adam didn't think he should ask for anything more.

Before debating the benefits of negotiating, I had Adam list the benefits he regarded as most important from his current Salary and Benefit Chart (see pages 148–149) to compare with those offered for the new position:

Current

⇨ **Salary**: $85,000

⇨ **Last bonus:** $7,000

⇨ **Health insurance**: Company covered 75 percent for $6,500 annual premium

⇨ **Vacation:** Four weeks, plus seven holidays

⇨ **401K retirement:** Employer contribution 6 percent

New Position

⇨ **Salary:** $100,000

⇨ **Estimated bonus:** Based on previous year, $12,000

⇨ **Health insurance:** Company contribution 80 percent of $6,500 annual premium

⇨ **Vacation:** Three weeks, plus seven holidays

⇨ **401K retirement:** Employer contribution 4 percent

Adam's Goals

After listing his current and future compensation package, I had Adam research salary ranges that existed for similar VP market research positions. His research revealed that the average salary for large companies was closer to $127,000 (not including bonus). This information put his circumstances in a realistic context, giving him the confidence to view the offer from a different perspective and ultimately request a higher salary. Adam realized he would take on greater responsibility in this job that entitled him to compensation commensurate for his field and position. With a clearer view of the big picture, Adam also took into consideration that he needed a wage that would allow him to live comfortably in Boston, where the cost of living is higher than Baltimore.

An additional compelling factor was his age. At forty-five years old, Adam was starting to look more seriously at retirement savings. In analyzing the offer, he noted the reduction in employer contribution and recognized the need to negotiate a percentage increase that would strengthen his retirement situation. We also made sure that Adam would be able to maintain his interests outside work, especially travel, so although the offer provides three weeks of vacation, Adam decided to negotiate for four.

Adam's Value to the Employer

To help solidify his confidence, I had Adam review his qualifications and experience relevant to the position. An MBA with eighteen years experience in technology market research, Adam began as a market research analyst and rose to senior market research manager. He is an expert in collecting and analyzing data on consumer insights that have successfully determined and outperformed projected sales of digital technology products. He also designed and introduced an interactive market research system that easily pulls out available customer data to accurately predict market trends—a system that particularly interests the hiring manager. Adam knows the combination of his experience, creative thinking, and sharp analytical skills can help this company launch new products that will generate high revenues. With a renewed sense of confidence and clarity about his strengths and value, Adam mapped out his terms for negotiation.

Adam's Ideal Package

⇨ **Salary:** $115,000 (mid-size company); **top priority**. (If the bonus nears $10,000, his total will be close to $125,000.)

⇨ **401K:** Employer contribution 6 percent

⇨ **Vacation:** Four weeks a year

⇨ **Lowest salary willing to accept**: $107,000

Adam's Negotiation Outline

Before moving on to practicing negotiations, I had Adam organize the content of his presentation using the negotiation outline.

⇨ **Confirmation:** Interest in the VP market research position.

⇨ **Salary research analysis:** Salary average of $128,000 in large companies for comparable positions, plus increase in cost of living.

⇨ **Benefit review:** Higher employer contribution (6 percent) for retirement plan and increased paid vacation.

⇨ **Priorities:** Salary (first); retirement (second); vacation (third).

⇨ **Personal market value:** Skills and knowledge that lead to success in sales and creation of new data system.

⇨ **Appreciation:** Thanking hiring manager for (hopefully) considering Adam's requests.

The Rehearsal

Once Adam identified the full range of priorities to be considered in the course of negotiations, we did some role-playing, with myself in the role of the employer.

Adam: Hello, this is Adam calling to discuss the market research position. I am very excited about the offer you extended for the vice president position at DigitExcel. I would like to discuss the offer if this is still a good time for you. (Confirmation)

Employer: Adam, good to hear from you. Are you ready to sign the offer? Do you have some questions?

Adam: After I received the full offer in writing, I spent some time researching salary ranges for VP of marketing research positions. Based on my research, your salary offer is over $25,000 below the average. I hope there is some room to negotiate the salary. (Salary Research)

Employer: Frankly, I am quite surprised that our salary is so much lower than our competitors. We pride ourselves on offering our employees a strong compensation package. Can you tell me more about your research?

Adam: Sure. According to the data I researched, the average salary for a vice president of market research is $128,000, reaching as high as $155,000 without including bonuses. Considering that DigitExcel is a mid-size company, along with the need for me to move to an area of increased living costs, I was looking at salary of $115,000. This, of course, does not mean that I am selling short my excitement about working for DigitExcel, nor does this minimize my admiration for the company's mission.

If you look at my considerable experience and how my particular skill in analyzing consumer insights on tech products has consistently driven revenue growth, I am confident that I will deliver similar, or better, results for DigitExcel. During our interview you noted that you were impressed with many of my innovative projects and results. At DigitExcel, I will be taking on greater responsibility along with the higher living costs I mentioned. (Salary Research Analysis, Personal Market Value, Confirmation)

Employer: I see your point, but I am not sure we can exactly meet your salary request. Did you carefully review our benefits package? We are very competitive. Perhaps that would make up for any perceived salary deficits.

Adam: I did review the benefits package, which is impressive! I contacted Robert in HR, who was helpful in answering my questions on the details of the various health plans. The benefit I would like to discuss is the 401(k) plan. I see that you contribute 4 percent toward retirement. My current employer contributes 6 percent. I am at a stage in life where saving for retirement is a priority, so I would appreciate it if you would consider increasing the contribution to 6 percent. I have four weeks of vacation where I am now and hope it's possible to increase my vacation time by an additional week. (Benefit Review)

Employer: We do have fixed percentage on 401(k) plans for all employees in the first year. But it is possible to increase the employer contribution closer to 5 percent in your second year. We might be able to give you a few more vacation days. Let me think about your benefit and salary request and get back to you by the end of the week. If we can't meet your salary, keep in mind we evaluate employee performance after six months, and if your performance is strong, we will offer a salary increase. And I will keep in mind your relocation and cost of living expenses.

Adam: I appreciate the consideration and understanding you are giving to my requests. I look forward to hearing from you later this week. (Appreciation)

When it came time for his real negotiation, Adam was prepared. With knowledge and self-assurance based on a thorough review of priorities and analysis of the compensation package, Adam was confident about asking for more. Further supported by a carefully rehearsed practice session, Adam articulated a strong case for negotiating a higher salary and benefits. He was able to do this in a manner that showed the employer they were hiring a person of substance who would be a valued advocate for the company. At the same time, he negotiated a more satisfying work situation that would bolster his self-respect. In the end, Adam pulled off the negotiations with flying colors, achieving a positive outcome all around.

The Final Offer

⇨ **Salary:** $108,500 (Salary to be reviewed in six months with possible 5 percent raise based on performance.)

⇨ **Relocation support:** $2,500

⇨ **Retirement contribution:** 4 percent first year, 5 percent second year

⇨ **Vacation:** Two extra days first year, four weeks second year

As satisfactory as these numbers sounded, Adam still did not rush to accept. With continued focus on his long-term goals, he asked the hiring manager to consider increasing the retirement contribution to 6 percent in the second year. The hiring manager agreed to review this in a year based on his performance. So although Adam initially resisted negotiating his offer, he ended up with an additional $11,000 plus two extra vacation days.

Negotiating Styles and Scenarios

No two negotiations are the same—after all, the dialogue is always between two distinct individuals, each with a personal style of communication. Here you'll find some advice on effective approaches to incorporate into your style—and some common pitfalls to avoid. Also included here are pointers on navigating negotiations with very different players: an extrovert or a fellow introvert. And what do you do if an employer won't budge on salary? We'll cover that, too.

Three Negotiation Style Mistakes

1. **Avoiding:** Adam's immediate instincts told him to just accept the offer as is or he might lose any chance of getting hired at all. Avoiding is a self-defeating style used to resist any situation hinting of a conflict. What should be avoided instead is playing to any deep-seated lack of self-esteem and that little voice inside that whispers negative thoughts. If you can just quiet that voice and put aside the rationalizations, you will be amazed at how much they do indeed want you.

2. **Accommodating:** When you hold the company's needs above all others, you naturally minimize your own and weaken your position. Introverts often fall prey to adopting the accommodating style of negotiation because they are quick to support and listen to the needs of others. Unfortunately, this style of negotiation can be as risk averse as the avoiding style. Don't give in at the first indication that the hiring manager is questioning your requests. Zero in on your priorities and negotiate with your ultimate goals in mind. When you focus on the employer's concerns, and consequently minimize your own needs and desires, you basically accommodate the employer at your own expense. In this scenario, you are likely to walk away from negotiations feeling disappointment and a sense of injustice.

3. **Compromising:** This negotiation style is based on making trades. For example, you might trade a salary increase for a type of benefit because you see it as a fair trade for the employer. When using the compromising style, each party gains something they want, but it can be a tricky process for the introvert. In particular, empathizing with the employer's needs may put your own priorities at risk. Although considering the employer's needs is not a bad approach, you may lose out on some terms that are priorities for you because you want to help out the employer.

Two Ideal Approaches

1. **Collaborating:** In this style of negotiating, you and the hiring manager work together toward a solution, rather than competing with one another by trading terms. Your role is to understand the hiring manager's challenges, and to look for solutions that incorporate each other's needs. The collaborating style is essentially a conversation that explores various options in search of an agreement—an understanding that meets the goals of each party as closely as possible, while avoiding a power struggle. This is a good exercise for future reference because the person you are collaborating with may become your direct supervisor. Use this style with diplomacy and clarity to establish a congenial precedent that models the respect you will show your supervisor, colleagues, and support staff when you come onboard in this new position.

2. **Employing strong, confident language:** Accept the fact that some butterflies will flutter in your stomach just before you present your negotiation points. It's only human considering that this process may affect your work life for the foreseeable future. Mask the nervousness by communicating your points in an assertive manner, using words that come across as both clear and strong. Avoid deflating expressions such as: "I feel that . . ." or "I just want to ask . . ." Instead, introduce phrases that speak to confidence, like: "At this point I would like to discuss . . ." or "My experience has made me certain that . . ." Using language that reflects strength and confidence engenders respect and admiration—which often leads to a positive response or outcome overall.

Negotiating With an Extrovert

Sometimes you psych yourself up for negotiations only to be confronted by the ultimate extrovert. In the face of your potential new boss's overt friendliness and hard-wired energy dominating the conversation, you turn

inward. You aren't sure when to break in, but this is not a good time to sub-
tract yourself from the equation. Instead, let your spirit rise to the occasion.
The best way to handle this potential scenario is by using reflective listening. This well-respected technique in humanistic psychology acknowledges
the speaker by commenting or restating what you heard your speaker say.

This method will help form a connection with the person who may
be your new boss and allow you to introduce your points for negotiation
such as salary, benefits, or work terms. Reflective listening can demand
your patience as well as a concerted effort to amiably speak up. Here's an
example of an introvert using this technique with an extrovert HR representative who had been going on for some time about specific challenges
in the department:

> Maria, I certainly understand the position you are in as you face the
> existing challenges in your department and the restrictions set by hu-
> man resources, especially where benefits are concerned. While not mini-
> mizing these issues, I would like to talk with you more about salary
> and see if there is a possibility of working at home at least once a week.

The fact is, reflective listening is natural for introverts. It allows you to
fall back on those valuable traits of your introverted personality—perceptive, observant, being a good listener—when negotiating with an ultra-
extroverted hiring manager. Using this technique, you can simultaneously
turn what you are hearing into respect for the speaker and advocacy for
your own needs and expectations. If anxiety rears its head as the extroverted manager takes over, avoid freezing up by taking a slow, deep reassuring
breath. Override all the verbiage by reminding yourself of your purpose
and goals. Then, find that relevant moment to jump in. Remember: At
some point, even an extrovert has to take a breath.

If you start on the right foot with an extrovert during negotiations, you
may find they form a strong bond with you.

Bargaining With an Introvert

A manager who leans toward introversion might open the conversation in a
friendly but reserved way. Instead of taking control of the conversation, the

manager might focus immediately on you and make sure that you fully understand the compensation package. Or they might get right to the point and ask if you have any questions or concerns.

After you present your points for negotiation, there may be a pause as the hiring manager thinks over your requests. Avoid the temptation to allay your nervousness by rushing in simply to fill the gap with sound. Allowing the silence will be far more productive than anything you might say and will give the hiring manager the necessary space to process the items just discussed. If it were you in their position, you too would appreciate a breather to gather your thoughts. In negotiations with an introvert, it is during this pause that the points you pitched may be under consideration. So let the introverted manager ponder without interruption; in the momentary silence, you may hear the sound of the cash register ringing!

The main advantage you have when negotiating with an introvert is that they listen to you uninterrupted, and you are likely to have enough space to sell your points. They may not respond or engage a lot, or they may even ask for more time to consider your requests, but this is no cause for concern. Just be patient.

Negotiations Breakdown: When Salary Won't Budge

There are situations in which the employer's hands are tied when it comes to bumping up your salary. If you really want the job, ask that your salary request be revisited after a few months, at least by six. By that time, you will have proven your value, and the organization will be more inclined to increase your salary to ensure your continued services. No employer wants to lose a top performer.

Also recognize when it's time to walk away. If you know you can't live on the salary or believe it is way below your experience and credentials, you won't be happy. Turning down an offer for good reasons also reflects self-respect. If you decide to decline the position, end the negotiations on a positive note, expressing your appreciation for their time, your respect and admiration for the company mission, and your regret for having to turn down the offer. You never know if you will run into the HR representative or manager in the future.

Negotiating as a Life Skill

As your career unfolds, your ability to negotiate will impact your potential to achieve your goals and the gains that you deserve. The more you take risks to negotiate with senior leaders and colleagues, the more your confidence will soar and fuel your power in the workplace. Your employer will view your ability to negotiate with respect, as well as a sign of self-confidence and skill. Even with preparation and practice, you may not always succeed, but you will continue to grow professionally and maintain a healthy self-esteem.

8
ONBOARD WITH FINESSE

Once you successfully negotiate the terms of your job offer, the real test begins in earnest. Starting work for a new employer can feel like plunging into a brave new world of unknowns. You will be thrown into an entirely new kind of negotiation as you learn to harmonize with different personalities, expectations, quirks, tempo, and style. What will your new boss be like? Will your colleagues be openly friendly and supportive? Or will they interact on a subtler level? What will it take to be a strong performer in this uncharted universe?

Having a more introverted style may create additional challenges and stress for you, especially in the rapid fire environment of the modern-day workplace that seems more suited to those with outgoing personalities. You may struggle at the starting gate with speaking up or taking the initiative with the boss or colleagues. It's best to balance these fears by being yourself and embracing the many good points of your introversion that have carried you this far. For example, as a valued listener who asks perceptive questions, you show an interest in learning and a genuine desire to include colleagues in your discussions. Your innate nature will also be a plus as you engage with coworkers on projects that demand focus, concentrated effort, and creative thinking. However, although it is okay to work quietly in your office, you need to find ways to communicate regularly and effectively with the staff beyond email and voicemail. Obviously, you are not at the office to be the life of the party, but you don't want to cut yourself off (as introverts have a tendency to do). All you need to do is learn to swim with the organizational flow.

Designed to help an introvert start off on the right foot from the very first day, this chapter features a seven-step plan for success, a blueprint for navigating the organizational landscape, communicating effectively with your supervisor and colleagues, and understanding appropriate workplace etiquette.

Start Out Right

The first few days on a new job could be awkward as you maneuver basic details and meet colleagues and office staff. It takes time to feel at home with the new faces and foreign environment that you are thrown into.

As you feel your way through those first days on the job, jot down impressions and notes on what will help you succeed in your daily work life. Documenting and organizing your observations can stop your mind from spinning and give you a greater understanding of what is happening around you, as well as inside your own head. You can break down your observations into two categories:

⇨ **New information:** Essential information that you have learned so far

⇨ **Questions:** What to ask to clarify your observations or new information

Being thoughtful and methodical, view the first weeks at a new job like a research project. Employ those keen observational and listening skills to get a feel for the company pulse and gain insight into job expectations. Be mindful of your boss's and colleagues' personalities, and determine the best ways to work with them.

Eventually, you will have to take the reins and demonstrate initiative, but in the early innings, being yourself and relying on your own strengths is the best strategy. In the first weeks, do what is natural: look, listen, and reflect.

Wipe the Slate Clean

Introverts have a tendency to take things to heart by internalizing failures or difficult experiences. If you allow these experiences to take control of your attitude, you threaten to sour an otherwise auspicious future. If you had a bad experience in the past with a manager or coworker, get it out of your system so it doesn't cloud your new work environment. Talk it out in your head, or have a dialogue with a trusted friend who can help you put things into perspective. Some honest self-reflection may reveal that you contributed to the perceived negative experience or that you might have done something different to ameliorate the situation. Make a pact with yourself to change your behavior if a similar situation arises, and adopt a positive outlook that will refresh and renew your work life. Begin your new work adventure with a clean emotional slate.

Understand the Organization

Whereas your homework for the interview included knowledge of the company's mission and vision, it's a good idea to dig deeper into the five-year or strategic plan because this provides a broader view of the company horizon. Study the organizational chart so you know where you stand in relation to the powers that be. Learn how one manager relates to another, what employees handle various responsibilities, and who reports to whom.

Read through the human resources employee handbook for information on company policy and procedures related to issues such as intellectual property; you will need to know when the company owns what you create on work time. So that you don't lose out on any benefits, become aware of important sign-up periods, as well as when you are qualified for certain benefits. Also, read up on the company resources (like computers or cell phones) to ensure that you don't violate company policy on usage.

Acronyms and Jargon

Acronyms abound in present-day society, so it's not surprising that many organizations use them in lieu of long-winded office or division titles. When I worked at the University of Pennsylvania, the career-planning office was known as CPPS (Career Planning and Placement Services) under the VPUL (Vice Provost for University Life).

Every field has special words or expressions unique to its industry that are often not understood by the general public. For example, jargon associated with investment banking includes "catching a falling knife," "Chinese wall," "EBITA," "Fire Drill," and "Roadshow." Getting up to speed on the language of your workplace will accelerate your adjustment and help you feel like a member of the club.

Social Graces

Your fellow professionals and clients will expect you to follow accepted rules of social interaction, common courtesy, appropriate dress, and respect for others. Pay attention to the social graces of your work culture, so you don't embarrass yourself by making faux pas like showing up for a formal business meeting in casual attire, or speaking disparagingly about a former boss's incompetence. Awareness of wardrobe expectations, proper business etiquette, and other such do's and don'ts can all contribute to how you integrate into a new corporate environment.

Etiquette

Workplace etiquette requires subtle observation. But this aspect of communication is just as important as understanding the main professional rules. First impressions can stick like super glue, so avoid interpersonal slip-ups by being courteous: "Please" and "thank you" are still in style; keep your cell phone on vibrate, and stay home if you are sick. Watch how respected colleagues in the office interact, and use their model of good behavior.

Wardrobe

Wear clothes in good taste but styles that initially lean on the conservative side. You may find that business casual is the acceptable office style, except when meeting with executives, board members, or important clients (during which more formal attire is expected). The definition of business casual is very fluid and varies wildly from office to office. Watch how senior-level staff and colleagues dress in your first few weeks; then, keep your own appearance in the same fashion ballpark. Eventually, you will figure out how to express your personality and personal fashion sense while respecting the often-unspoken office dress code.

Group Dynamics

Become acquainted with the organization's personality, and get your finger on the pulse of workplace norms to help you acclimate to your new surroundings. At department or division staff meetings, observe what issues are raised and how the leader facilitates and manages the group. Scan the room to see how staff react, both verbally and in their facial expressions, body language, and gestures. Is the climate one of enthusiasm and genuine engagement, or do employees seem detached and disinterested, drumming their fingers, yawning, and glancing at cell phones?

Time in the staff lounge or around the coffee machine can provide important learning opportunities. When your colleagues are relaxed, they will be more apt to speak freely and offer their true impressions on company programs and initiatives, so pay attention. You can also gain valuable information on staff members at varying levels of seniority and discover what feelings they inspire among their coworkers.

Schedules

In the orientation phase, keep your periscope high and discretely observe norms in the office. Do your coworkers generally maintain a nine-to-five schedule, or do they tend to work long hours and take work home? Are your peers taking lunch breaks or eating at their desks? This is not simply a question of having to conform. It is a matter of recognizing the realities of your new position to ensure that you keep up with the expected pace and output of work.

Performance Expectations

Crucial to your success in the first few weeks is the energy and attention you devote to communication with your immediate supervisor. At the earliest possible opportunity, take the initiative to begin a dialogue with your boss about the best way to exchange information. For example, when questions require a rapid response, does your boss prefer email or a more open-door policy and personal approach? With that three-to-six-month probation period hanging over your head, you'll want to find out as soon as possible the needs of your company and your boss and the best way to deliver them. Make sure you have a clear understanding of expectations and responsibilities and how your performance will be measured. This might also be an opportune time to ask your boss for advice on the organization's key players; such individuals might help you improve your performance in fulfilling your role, as well as warn you of pitfalls to avoid.

Colleagues: Their Pivotal Role in Your Work Life

Researchers at Tel Aviv University examined and tracked the health of 820 working adults throughout a period of twenty years, starting with a health exam as a baseline.[1] The results of the study showed the factor most closely linked to maintaining good health was supportive coworkers. So, as you tap into that extroverted energy to make a new work environment your own, use some to establish congenial relationships with your coworkers.

Remember: You are not just functionaries but real people who benefit from socialization. Don't wait for an engraved invitation. Get up, go over, smile, and say hello. No one will see you as bothersome if you start off with the most basic comments such as, "How long have you worked here?" or "What are your main responsibilities?" This is an unthreatening way to establish rapport and makes for a comfortable start from which you can graduate into other personal questions such as, "How was your weekend?" Take stock of the high performers in the office versus the office complainers and work avoiders. A good-natured and highly respected employee can be invaluable when showing you the tricks of the trade and how to avoid missteps.

Loneliness

It's perfectly normal to feel as if you are stranded on an island during the first weeks at a new job. This type of loneliness is a temporary state and has nothing to do with introversion or personality type. Even if you are making the effort to meet the staff, it takes time and experiences to form meaningful connections and establish comfortable interactions with fellow employees. Also, beware that some colleagues may have formed cliques. Don't waste your efforts trying to break into groups that have already established a strong bond; instead, keep your feelers out for someone who seems to click with you or reaches out to help you with a question or task. A friendly connection with just one person in the office can alleviate feelings of loneliness.

A gradual approach to cultivating relationships should appeal to you as an introvert, because it provides the opportunity to create far more meaningful connections than simply diving head first into the crowd. Conveniently, one of the best strategies to become an accepted team member fits perfectly with your nature.

During this period of job transition, reach out to family and friends for some extra support. No matter how much focus and time you devote to the new job's demands, continue to engage in those familiar activities and outlets that make you feel part of an established group or community. Friends and outside activities will reinforce your ability to successfully cultivate relationships both at your workplace and beyond.

Strategy Officer Connects With an Executive Leader

Marc had aspired to work at the Gates Foundation since graduating college ten years prior, so landing a job there as a senior strategy officer was a dream come true. His first few weeks on the job seemed to be going well, but he didn't feel that he was establishing strong relationships with colleagues or the executive team. Meanwhile, his boss was encouraging but occupied with multiple projects. As a person who naturally leans toward introversion, he began to retreat more and more to his office and felt increasingly isolated. He finally realized that he would have to fuel his social energy and make more of an effort to initiate conversation at work. Of course, this realization only heightened his concerns about fitting in, adding to his list of worries.

However, the next day he stepped into the elevator and noticed Henna, the deputy director of program advocacy, and introduced himself. From researching the senior team at the foundation, he remembered that Henna was a fellow alum of Indiana University. He mentioned this, which sparked an engaging conversation about their common experiences at the university. Then Henna asked Marc how he was adjusting to his new job and suggested that they go to lunch in a few weeks. She also offered to answer questions or provide any information about her division that Marc would find helpful. In this instance, Marc made a fortuitous decision to override the silence of the elevator and introduce himself to a senior executive, thus cultivating a relationship with an important professional leader and potential mentor.

Why New Hires Often Fail

A recent three-year study conducted by Leadership IQ, a global leadership training and research company, found that 46 percent of newly hired employees fail within eighteen months, while only 19 percent achieve unequivocal success.[2] According to the study, this failure is not the result of weak technical skills. The primary reason new hires fail is poor interpersonal skills because of their inability to manage emotions, reluctance to accept feedback, and lack of motivation and initiative. With these issues in mind, don't let yourself become a statistic. Use the power of your introversion to carefully listen and observe. Use your emotional intelligence, or EI (capacity to recognize your own and others' emotions), to communicate with colleagues and senior leaders throughout your crucial probationary period. Follow this seven-step plan, and you will be on your way to joining the successful 19 percent who move forward as valued employees.

A Seven-Step Plan for Success: The First Sixty to Ninety Days

Taking advantage of your personal style, you absorbed and learned how to navigate important aspects of your role and the workplace culture. You survived the first weeks of your new job, and now it's time to take a more active role. Your success in the first quarter of a new job will depend greatly on your ability to build effective working relationships with senior-level managers, colleagues, clients or customers, and support staff. Showing interest and initiative in assigned projects and specific responsibilities is equally important. Don't be shy about offering input and suggestions that may solve problems or promoting ideas that can further the success of the organization. Whether or not your contributions are adopted, you will begin to project yourself as an ally and committed team player.

Step One: Build a Relationship With Your Manager

Your number-one priority is to establish a productive relationship with your boss. As you get to know each other, find subjects in common that will help break the ice. Whether a hobby, children, sports, or theater interests, the most mundane topic can lead to chemistry that spills over into a positive working relationship. Maybe you share an interest in tennis or film, or have children of the same age. By establishing this kind of commonality, you naturally foster an easy and ongoing dialogue with your boss. You can then check in on your common interests at the beginning or end of meetings or stop by the office occasionally for a short chat. It is not expected that you and your manager will be best friends. Rather, aim to develop this delicate relationship with the goal of working together in ways that benefit the company.

Show Empathy

Managers have their own set of demands, ranging from creating and executing strategic plans to increasing revenue to ensuring that teams meet important project deadlines or quotas. As an introvert, you are sensitive to others' needs, so you can use this trait to express empathy with your manager. Reassure your manager that you are aware of the responsibility your new tasks hold, and you are willing to contribute toward accomplishing the same goals.

As you learn more about your manager's priorities, look for opportunities to provide support or assistance. If you are ready, you might offer to take something off your manager's plate or propose relevant suggestions that might prove helpful. Serve as a partner to achieve an important goal to show that you can be a positive force. This makes your boss look good and it establishes you as vital member of the team.

Freezing Up

If your reserved, introverted side takes over and you are nervous about what to say in initial meetings with your boss, tap into your curiosity in advance, and prepare some thoughtful questions about your responsibilities or the organization. This will both relax your nerves and leave a good first impression that you have been thinking seriously about your work. Ask your boss the following questions to help you understanding your role, your manager, and the organization.

⇨ What would you like me to accomplish in the first quarter?

⇨ What major challenges are you facing, and how can I help?

⇨ What are the most important lessons I should learn in the next few months to be successful?

⇨ What changes or current trends in the organization should I be aware of?

⇨ What types of issues do you want consultation or final approval on?

⇨ What other staff can help me get oriented?

⇨ What should I know about your work and management style?

Take Charge With a Hands-Off Manager

Managers are preoccupied and focused on a myriad of issues that existed long before you came on board. Your manager may have a deficit of attention when it comes to delegating responsibilities or ensuring that new staff are thoroughly briefed and oriented. In fact, your otherwise competent manager may not be the best communicator. Be proactive and ready to paddle your own boat when you sense that you are being left at sea. Determine if there are any basic tasks that need completing, and take the initiative to attack them on your own.

Once you have a better understanding of the manager's personality and priorities, and of the division mission and goals, suggest a project that you can pursue on your own. Use your ingenuity to determine how you can be of assistance. Every manager has an Achilles' heel—yours may not have the most robust skills as a facilitator or natural leader. If this is the case, your boss will be relieved to have an employee who is an independent thinker and offers ideas on how to help them and the organization. With a non-communicator, it's best to use an extroverted approach to ensure a streaming dialogue and maintain a connection in order to complete important projects or resolve dicey issues.

Step Two: Build Relationships With Coworkers

It is realistic to expect that some of the new coworkers to whom you introduce yourself may turn into lifelong relationships. You may even stay in contact with some of these supportive colleagues after you move on to other positions. To this day, I am in contact with several colleagues I worked with throughout my career. Their welcome expertise helped extend my career, while their emotional support was equally valuable.

Engage in the Five-Minute Conversation

As with many of the tasks mentioned previously, a sturdy framework for positive relationships with coworkers can be constructed with some thoughtful advanced planning. So take five! Five *minutes,* that is, to have a conversation with a few coworkers for a short chat. Stop by their offices in the morning, at lunchtime, or another appropriate time for small talk. Limit the discussion to noncontroversial or uncomplicated topics. If you aren't good at small talk, start with one of the three W's: the weather, the weekend, or the world—and avoid politics and religion. You don't want your attempt at reaching out to result in a burned hand. Very often, a brief visit and short chat can lead to a lunch or coffee get-together, or even an idea for collaborating on a work project.

Although in-person conversations tend to be the ideal approach for building relationships, you can also take advantage of social media to get to know a colleague. For instance, if you notice that a coworker posted a professional article or comment on LinkedIn or Twitter, you can show interest by responding to the post. This approach works well for a shy introvert who would rather initiate a connection from behind a computer screen. This often establishes the groundwork for an eventual face-to-face relationship in which one can continue the initial online discussion and form a more meaningful connection.

Balance Your Emotions

The first few months in any new environment can cause the adrenaline to flow and the ears to perk up. The key is not to appear defensive. Instead, minimize your fears by reminding yourself of past achievements and the fact that it takes time to adjust to a new work environment. If one of your coworkers makes a condescending or critical comment, stay calm even if you feel hurt and want to retaliate. Take a deep breath and realize this person doesn't really know you and may simply be the office nudge. Whatever the reason, too much speculation, however reasonable, can be debilitating. Bottom line: It is simply too early in the game to take anything to too personally. You are just not that important in the context of this new environment . . . yet!

After you process the interaction with the coworker, try to see the humor in the incident. Keep a wide berth from this coworker for a time and devote your attention to those who seem genuinely interested in their work and in getting to know you as a colleague. Professionalism, not feeding into office intrigue and drama, should be your mantra for the sake of your current and long-term career development. Focus on the pride and satisfaction in your work rather than distractions from interpersonal miscues. That will help take the edge off those initial, sometimes shaky, ninety days. Projecting a positive, willing attitude will be the best kind of invitation for coworkers to collaborate with you. Be the soul of optimism and you will build a bridge that reaches staff and coworkers alike.

Step Three: Build Relationships With Administrative Support Staff

Naturally, as a new employee working to perform your tasks effectively, you look for ways to demonstrate your capabilities to your boss and coworkers. Of course, it is only normal to want to impress those who are evaluating you. But don't overlook the importance of developing strong relationships with support staff. The receptionist, administrative assistants, and volunteers are great allies. If you show them respect, they can make your job easier.

Your boss and coworkers lean heavily on support staff for help in managing major projects and the day-to-day operations. Meanwhile, the administrative staff are in a front-row position to observe how you go about your work and interact with customers, clients, and other staff members. If you show signs of being unprofessional, they are also in a position to give their impressions of you to the boss. Create a harmonious relationship with administrative staff, and it's likely that they will support you in completing work projects and meeting crucial deadlines. Extend your goodwill to janitors and facility maintenance personnel for similar reasons, and because it is the sign of a decent and caring person.

Step Four: Meet Key Players

First impressions stick like glue. In the first quarter of your new position, make it your goal to get to know the senior leadership and star performers. Try to schedule brief informational meetings with key players to learn more about their roles within the company and how they put it into action. If you strategically set up less formal face-to-face introductions, this will be less intimidating than meeting them for the first time at a division meeting or large event. In keeping with your introvert's psyche, have relevant, appropriate questions prepared when you meet with any key leader.

These preliminary days provide a rare opportunity to employ your natural ability to listen and empathize, to learn how those above you reached their position, and what motivates and inspires them. It begins with that all-important first impression and verbal interaction. Remember: You can enhance this dialogue if you also discover something in common.

Questions to Ask a Key Player

⇨ What is your main function?

⇨ What are your major responsibilities?

⇨ How long have you worked for the company?

⇨ What do you enjoy about your work?

⇨ What are your major challenges?

⇨ Where do you see the company moving in the next five years?

⇨ What's your general advice on how to succeed in this company?

Step Five: Acknowledge Others

You have entered a new universe, so it won't surprise your boss, assistant, or colleague if you require some clarification or direction. Be up front about your desire to do the right thing the right way, and when a colleague or supervisor addresses your questions or offers a helping hand, be sure to express your genuine appreciation. After all, everyone likes to be acknowledged from time to time for a job well done. Compliment your boss if you were impressed by the way they spearheaded a project or handled a conflict. Similarly, let a coworker know how much you learned and were inspired by their patience and skill in handling a difficult client. Understand that these are not simply gestures; they are hallmarks of an employee who has character and a supportive spirit that recognizes the accomplishments of others. In short, expressing appreciation can be key to developing positive relationships in your office.

Step Six: Watch Your Communication

Your ability to interact harmoniously with others and express your thoughts and ideas in a cogent way will impact your success and determine how the staff reacts to you. Introverted energy can be an asset as you listen carefully to others and think before you speak. These positive qualities can help establish trusting relationships with senior leaders, coworkers, clients, and customers.

Meetings

In the first few months, the thought of speaking up at meetings and finding that perfect moment to communicate your ideas might seem risky. As a guide to organizing your thoughts, prepare in advance a short agenda or a bulleted list with updates on your projects or assignments. Include any ideas, concerns, or questions you have before a major staff or division meeting.

You may not be ready to volunteer information or answer questions at the first or second meeting, but you will eventually need to comment or offer an opinion. Of course, you don't have to be the first one to speak; it's perfectly fine to listen carefully and get a sense of the meeting's climate before you dive in. As you get to know the staff and become more familiar with the rhythm of these meetings, you will find it easier to participate.

Eventually, you will be asked a question or put on the spot for information that may leave you feeling flummoxed. But no one has the right answer on the tip of the tongue 100 percent of the time. You can always circle back to your manager or coworker with comments once you have had some time to review and reflect.

Emails and Texting

In the modern workplace, a great deal of communication is channeled through email. You are now more accessible than ever with the added pressure of responding to your sender's request as soon as possible. Since you are trying to make a good impression in the first ninety days, answer work-related emails promptly. And today, it's not just your inner circle of office staff with whom you need to effectively interact. You also want to make a good impression on customers or clients.

The content of your emails and texts should always relate to professional issues. Watch your tone, avoid slang and clichés, and never use email or text to sort out interpersonal or work-related conflicts. Sensitive issues can easily be misconstrued in writing and intensify misunderstandings. In cyberspace, nothing is truly confidential, so don't ever discuss legal or other highly sensitive matters through email or texts. It is crucial, particularly in the first ninety days, to review all messages carefully for content, misspellings, and grammatical errors, and to demonstrate a careful competence.

Step Seven: Appraise Your Own Performance

As you become familiar with the prevailing cultural norms and your designated responsibilities, take a personal inventory during your first sixty to ninety days that reflects your performance so far. Be honest, but also fair to yourself. Be sure to give yourself high marks for effort and credit for managing to survive the first month of your new job. Focus on your strengths and how you can capitalize on these to support the organization while furthering your career. Gauge your biggest challenges and identify ways you can fulfill these demands with available resources and the support of amenable staff.

SCORE: A Method for Self-Appraisal

I created SCORE to help my clients come up with an organized method for reviewing their performance in the first sixty to ninety days. SCORE helps you identify your strong points as well as the areas in which you can exercise improvement. It also helps you create an action plan for your new job by recognizing available opportunities and tapping into existing resources. Reviewing your self-assessment chart in Chapter 2 can give you some additional insight as you complete your self-appraisal and contribute to racking up a healthy SCORE. The process breaks down as follows:

⇨ **S–Strengths:** Identify your technical abilities, knowledge, and interpersonal skills that support the responsibilities of the position. What have you accomplished so far that tips the scales in your favor and has established you as a go-to employee?

⇨ **C–Challenges:** List factors that deserve your attention and the knowledge needed to cultivate further success. Highlight potential conflicts that might develop with colleagues or managers, and concerns you might have regarding projects or basic responsibilities.

⇨ **O–Opportunity:** Envision work projects or tasks that interest you. What are some of the evolving and creative ways that you could add value to the organization and continue to build your brand?

⇨ **R–Resources:** What people or resources are available to help you achieve and succeed? How might you benefit from the expertise of specific senior leaders and pertinent colleagues? How can you bring your external professional network into play on your path to success? Does your database require updating? What about financial resources? Do you need more funding for an ongoing project?

⇨ **E–Evaluation:** Summarize and evaluate what priority in the immediate future would help you succeed in your new job. Set priorities and create an action plan.

Lucinda Uses the SCORE Method to Determine Her Focus

Let's examine how SCORE helped Lucinda assess her performance and challenges, leading her to single out projects that support the mission of the organization. Lucinda accepted a position as director of community relations for a large retail chain. She made it through the first thirty days observing, asking questions, taking on basic responsibilities, and figuring out how to fit into the culture of her new organization. When it came time to move forward with certain projects, however, Lucinda felt unsure about where to start and how to fire up and manage her small staff.

Lucinda had several projects and programs on her plate, including the company's sponsorship of one of the largest 6K runs in the city, an employee volunteer project, and the company's charitable giving program. Although Lucinda tends to be reserved, the time she spent getting to know staff members using her keen observational skills served her well. Lucinda discovered early on that the company faced some morale issues and programmatic challenges. The employee volunteer program, for example, was a sticking point because it had not been successful in the past. And although the company was sporadically involved in charitable giving, there was no real established philosophy or ongoing strategic plan for philanthropy. These demands, among others, excited her sense of challenge, but also caused her to feel unsure about where to channel her energy for maximum effect.

Using the SCORE method, Lucinda was able to make the most of her introverted energy to think through the nature of these new demands, as well as possible remedies for the challenges presented. By calmly channeling her methodical thinking skills, she designed a realistic plan that would help her determine which projects to pursue. After coming up with a reasonable strategy, she moved on to the last stage of SCORE, implementing her action plan.

See how Lucinda broke down the elements of the SCORE process and how her strengths, challenges, potential opportunities, and available resources all led her to a forward-thinking evaluation.

S–Strengths

⇨ Cultivating relationships with staff at all levels and diverse groups in the community.

⇨ Thinking analytically and strategically.

⇨ Developing and implementing projects.

⇨ Creating and executing new programs.

⇨ Working with the media.

⇨ Creative thinking.

⇨ Researching and synthesizing information.

C–Challenges

⇨ Where to start and prioritize tasks.

⇨ How to motivate staff to work on employee volunteer program.

⇨ How to design and work with executive team to develop charitable giving strategy.

⇨ Manage large breast cancer 6K run.

⇨ Build relationships in the community.

O–Opportunity

⇨ *Employee Volunteer Program:* Evaluate key problems and rebuild the program. This will help the company's community image and offer a rewarding experience for employees, which will also enhance the organization's morale.

⇨ *Strategic Plan for Charitable Giving:* I believe that this is at the heart of the job. I can help the organization create a vision for this program that will allow me to educate and work closely with senior executives to benefit the local community.

R–Resources

⇨ Meet with a colleague in my network who has experience in my field.

⇨ Schedule time to meet with company leaders in human resources and marketing.

⇨ Review data on past events and programs.

⇨ Schedule meetings with leaders in the nonprofit community.

E–Evaluation

After an overall assessment of my personal strengths and the challenges presented, I pinpointed two projects that would benefit the organization and use my talents:

1. *External Community:* Charitable Giving Plan

2. *Internal Community:* Employee Volunteer Program

My goal is to set up a meeting with my boss (the vice president of communications) to present an agenda that features my project initiatives. To ensure a productive meeting, I will prepare an outline to guide me through my discussion with the vice president.

Outcome

Lucinda met with her boss, who was enthusiastic about her ideas regarding the two projects, but concerned that Lucinda might be taking on too much. Her boss recommended that she focus her energy on the strategic plan for charitable giving. He also offered valuable suggestions as to how to approach the senior executive team regarding envisioning and inaugurating a strategic plan. Lucinda was excited about the encouragement she received and requested that they meet on a regular basis so the project could benefit from her boss's continued insight, advice, and expertise. Linda's thoughtful preparation helped her attain the boss's support, resulting in an opportunity to move forward on a major organizational priority.

An Alternate Ending

Although the scenario between Lucinda and her boss had a favorable outcome, you may encounter a situation in which your new boss is skeptical about your readiness to proceed on a project or take on a responsibility. To increase the chances that at least one of your ideas gets approved, come into the discussion with two or three viable options. Put aside feelings of dejection if your manager nixes your idea completely or feels it may be too soon for you to handle ambitious projects. Don't give up. Move forward with a positive attitude about your existing responsibilities and prove you're a high performer. Continue to collect data, or read up on current relevant trends, then present your idea in a new framework at a later time. Time will establish trust based on your work ethic and performance. And your additional research may provide the hard data needed for a "Yes" instead of a "You better wait on that."

The Extroverted Manager

Energetic, talkative, and highly engaged in conversation, an extroverted manager can seem overpowering to your cool and reserved nature. But try to expand your thinking about extroversion and embrace your differences. Even if you aren't ready to respond to all of your manager's talking points, your facial expressions and active listening should show that you are paying attention and are ready to cooperate. An extrovert may feel uncomfortable if you are verbally nonresponsive and may mistake you for aloof or passive. Keep in mind that extroverts tend to talk and think at the same time, and easily take initiative. These qualities are helpful because they guarantee a substantial response to your questions or concerns.

To successfully work with an extrovert boss, take the initiative to up-date him or her regularly—don't wait for requests to check in about what's going on. And avoid long emails; extroverts would rather talk it out than respond with an equally long missive. When you do meet with an extrovert, preparation will help you overcome uncertainties. Plan ahead for what's on your mind; jot down some notes or create an agenda in advance. Pose direct questions on issues for which you need answers. This will prevent a mind freeze from the avalanche of your boss's verbiage and keep you from disappearing into the depths of the discussion. Your boss will appreciate your readiness by your thoughtful commentary and questions.

Depending on your comfort level and the extent to which you have connected with the new boss, you can share aspects of your introversion that provide a better understanding of your communication style. Let your boss know that you may seem quiet and a bit reserved at times, but this doesn't indicate your disinterest. Open up about the fact that you tend to process important issues first before putting them into words, and that you work carefully and methodically. Remember: A good manager wants to know the best ways to work with an employee, too. An honest assessment of your personal style may help your boss refrain from pushing too hard for an immediate response or quick, frantic action. Understanding each other's working tempo can lead to both an easier relationship and workplace success.

Gig, Solo Practitioners, and Virtual Workers

If you work virtually, getting to know personalities that work around you in cyberspace can be challenging, and it might be difficult to bond with your boss, coworkers, and clients. This is where the accelerated age of technology rears its head again. Even when you work solo, you can still build rapport with the people in your organization and connect successfully with clients using the endless tentacles of technology in a creative way. You can achieve this by following many of the suggestions in the seven-step plan. Introverts can be seduced by the peace, quiet, and solitude presented by working on their own, but this kind of seduction comes with the potential pitfall of becoming out of touch and isolated.

Cell phones and email provide a forum for discussing relevant issues and keeping important work contacts up to date. Introverts tend to thrive on face-to-face contact, so if you favor this type of communication, use FaceTime, Skype, and web conferencing to see each other's faces and get a better idea of who you are working with. Even though you are not on-site, you can resolve any conflicts or misunderstanding through direct conversation using a mobile device.

I once met a contract worker who formed a web group called "office time" with fellow contract workers. They meet virtually on the web once or twice a week, so although they are physically in different places, they work and chat with each other in an attempt to duplicate the in-person office experience.

Kendra Takes Steps to Fit In at Her New Job

Kendra was a successful graphic artist at a small advertising agency, but despite many positive factors, the company offered no opportunities for advancement or contribution to larger-scope projects. These dead-end realities spurred Kendra to look for more challenging positions, and she quickly landed a job at a large corporate advertising firm as the senior graphic designer.

After her initial optimism and excitement, she felt deflated by various obstacles to fitting into this new culture and the daunting task of designing projects for Fortune 500 clients. By the time Kendra contacted me for advice, she was convinced that she was faltering and would never make it on the big stage.

The first step was to help Kendra recognize that some anxiety and uncertainty are normal during a transition period. Kendra deserved the luxury of slowing down and letting time perform its magic, then taking gradual, small steps along this very new path. To rebuild her confidence, we shifted the discussion to focus on her past achievements. Then we came up with a strategy that would help her relax and feel more at ease in her new work environment.

Accomplishments

Kendra was the recipient of a design award in college and, more recently, a national award from Graphic Design USA. To put her present circumstances in perspective, we reviewed her relationships with the previous employer. Kendra acknowledged that she worked harmoniously with her colleagues and that her design work was so effective that clients often requested her to work on new projects.

Current Challenge

To adjust to the fast-paced, outgoing culture, she had to embrace her introverted style while introducing some extroverted actions. Kendra was freezing up at meetings and felt unable to contribute or generate ideas in sessions with colleagues and senior staff. These first meetings gave her a sense that she didn't belong, leaving her feeling unnerved and immobilized.

I suggested that Kendra not worry so much about pouring forth ideas just yet. Instead, I recommended that she use her introverted style to pose relevant questions that would help her develop an understanding of project goals and elemental issues. By asking these questions, she would be able to speak up and show interest.

At the next meeting, Kendra exercised active listening and injected pertinent questions into a brainstorming session for a new client's project. This exercise allowed her to have a clear picture of the project's demands and goals. After the meeting, Kendra reflected on the project and came up with a design concept. She showed the design to her boss, who was so impressed that he asked Kendra to present her graphic at the next staff meeting. After the initial "yes" moment, however, Kendra felt a new form of anxiety as she contemplated the reality of making such a bold presentation to the staff.

Outcome

To allay her anxiety, I asked Kendra to consider her coworkers and tailor her style of presentation to what she had learned about them so far, as well as to the client's goals. Kendra came up with a creative digital presentation narrating a story about the graphic that she believed would appeal to the client. I also encouraged Kendra to make a short list of bullet points that she could refer to if she lost her train of thought during her presentation. Despite her initial nail-biting, the presentation came off brilliantly, and she basked in positive feedback and compliments from the staff.

This early victory marked a major step toward solidifying good relations with her boss and colleagues. To reach this result, Kendra embraced her introverted strengths while exercising extroverted skills, such as showing interest in staff meetings by asking pertinent questions. These skills allowed her to take reasonable risks that yielded a significant reward in the end.

SURVIVE AND THRIVE

You may be competent at your job, but make sure you aren't toiling away in a bubble. Reflection is an asset in many contexts, but turning inward is a mistake when it comes to your career. Don't assume that busy coworkers and managers will recognize the fine work you are doing. It is equally self-defeating to shy away from discussing work problems with supervisors or colleagues. Make sure that you become a known quantity, or you will likely lose out on deserved recognition that leads to promotions and a future pay raise.

Volatility and change are the hallmarks of the present accelerated workplace. In this fast-lane environment, introverts need to make a concerted effort to go beyond their reserved nature and take the chance of standing up and being counted. You have a lot to contribute when it comes to important issues and the development of concepts and ideas that further the organization's mission. To achieve this, you can use means comfortable within the confines of your own personality to promote your talents and skills, while challenging yourself to speak up more.

In this chapter, you'll discover tools and techniques that will strengthen your outlook and help you dial up your career, plus tips for advancing your communications skills and taking actions that will get you noticed and receive the admiration of your peers and senior leaders.

Manage a Thriving Career

Once your career is up and running, you need to keep it healthy and moving forward; it won't maintain its momentum without your help. There are still areas you can pursue to strengthen your position, such as setting short-term goals, using your talents to their best advantage, solving problems, and meeting experts in your field. It is also recommended that you continue your education and training whenever possible, support a strong network, and keep your resume and LinkedIn profile up to date.

Your Compass

As with all aspects of life, it's impossible to predict with certainty how your career will evolve. But having some clear ideas of what you want to do and where you want to end up will increase the likelihood of getting to your destination.

A variety of factors can impact your career destiny, such as how you are presently situated—whether you are in your first job or have already reached the senior management level. Lifestyle issues can also affect your career's direction, such as parenthood, health considerations, or economic needs. As you clarify your priorities, combine your daydreams with logic as you ponder your long-term goals. Start with a grand vision and then whittle it down to more realistic objectives.

You can gain some control of your career and a bird's eye view into the future by booting up your personal GPS, which can chart potential career milestones and attainable goals.

Make Your Dreams Come True—
One Step at a Time

You may have a vision of becoming a manager or an aspiration to move up to a senior executive level. Or perhaps you have the courage and energy to consider leaving your current professional life as an employee and starting your own business. If you decide to break away and enter an entirely new field, you need to acquire relevant new information or obtain a specific educational degree. Even with a desire to remain in the same field, you need to expand your knowledge base.

Whatever your long-term plan, avoid discouragement and confusion by breaking down a large goal into small, achievable pieces. It also helps to set up manageable targets along the way. For example, if your goal is to advance to a higher-level position, you can take the lead on an upcoming project or demonstrate your expertise by presenting a seminar at a professional meeting or conference. These are professional activities that will exhibit your ability to initiate and lead while providing you the experience and skills associated with moving up the ranks.

Write Down Your Goals

Introverts are deep thinkers, so use that ability to write out a plan to achieve your goal. This is a perfect exercise for introverts and a process that has been shown to firmly fix your mission in your mind and increase the chances of accomplishing your objective.

Gail Matthews, a psychology professor at California's Dominican University, conducted a study on written goals using a sample of 267 people with diverse career backgrounds. She divided her sample into two groups: One simply *thought* about their goals, whereas a second group wrote them down. The study found that those who wrote down their goals experienced a significantly higher level of success in achieving them than those who did not write them down.[1] When you write, you send active signals to the left hemisphere of the brain—the side where logic resides. As a result, your consciousness tends to see the words as "written in stone" and takes serious note of your intention to accomplish them. To help stimulate your brain and stick to your mission, use the following formula for organizing and mapping out short-term goals.

⇨ **Specific short-term goal:** Your objective and what you want to achieve

⇨ **Timeline:** A general timeframe or deadline to achieve the goal

⇨ **Actions:** What you need to do to accomplish the goal

⇨ **Measure:** How you will measure your success

⇨ **Evaluation:** What is working and what needs to be modified

Charles Sets a Short-Term Goal: Achieve Career Advancement

The career aspiration of Charles, an IT project manager, is to advance to a higher-level position. To demonstrate his readiness and capability to reach the next level, Charles made "improvement of leadership skills" a dedicated short-term goal. His goal plan worksheet broke down as follows:

⇨ **Specific goal:** To strengthen leadership skills.

⇨ **Timeline:** Over the period of one year. To be reviewed in the first six months and follow up six months later.

⇨ **Actions:**

   ⇨ Meet with supervisor to review actions and gain support.

   ⇨ Train and supervise the summer intern: design orientation as well as generate and provide lists of tasks and resources.

   ⇨ Train new staff in department on database and division computer programs.

   ⇨ Lead meeting on an innovative trend in artificial intelligence (AI); create PowerPoint presentation.

   ⇨ Fill in for manager while she is away on vacation.

   ⇨ Apply for and attend internal leadership training program.

⇨ **Measure:**

   ⇨ Ask for feedback from intern and new staff on their training experience.

   ⇨ Survey staff through anonymous evaluation form for response to formal presentation on new AI trend.

   ⇨ Secure manager's evaluation of leadership skills.

   ⇨ Apply and assess new knowledge and skills from leadership training program.

⇨ **Evaluation:**

    ⇨ Received positive feedback from manager and colleagues on office technology training and handling of manager's responsibilities while she was away on vacation.

    ⇨ According to team feedback, need to improve delivery of presentation, providing more verbal explanation and relying less on PowerPoint slides.

    ⇨ Based on supervisor's recommendation, need to continue to increase leadership skills and become well versed in company's annual report.

Charles successfully achieved most of his short-term goals based on the positive feedback he received regarding the intern supervision and training new staff on office technology. He used his introverted energy to ask questions and get to know his intern, and the new staff sensed that Charles was invested in helping them learn the office computer programs. His boss expressed appreciation for how well Charles filled in for her during her vacation. However, the staff that attended his presentation reported that Charles depended too much on the PowerPoint slides in his delivery, so Charles will work on improving his public speaking skills for presentations in future.

Overall, Charles succeeded in building his leadership skills. In the end a higher-level position didn't materialize at his company, but he was offered an excellent position as a senior project manager at another reputable company where he will supervise a team of six and take on some exciting and challenging projects.

Tap Into Your Talents and Interests

One of the surest ways to clear for your career takeoff is to ensure that your work is a natural outlet for your abilities, and that your talents and passion are in harmony with the organization's needs. Introverts can thrive in any workplace, but only if they stay current and relevant. Pick a concept or idea that will add value to your professional profile and take initiative by integrating it into aspects of your work. Gather the very latest information, develop the concept as much as possible, and present it as a fully fleshed-out proposal to your boss or teammates.

Susanne, a psychologist working with veterans who suffer from post traumatic stress disorder (PTSD), is a perfect example. A creative thinker and writer, Susanne enjoys learning and applying new therapies and innovative techniques that result in positively transforming a person's life. She recently attended a workshop on a new treatment for PTSD and was encouraged by the results of this promising new approach. Utilizing this treatment, Susanne created a new program for PTSD for her agency that received attention, not just from the director of her unit, but also from other psychologists in her professional association and network. News of her success spread nationally, and she was approached by *Psychology Today* to write a monthly online column on the topic of veterans and PTSD. Her passion for learning and her talent for writing combined with action led to recognition and an exciting new opportunity.

Solve a Problem

The workplace is a popular place for unaddressed issues calling out for solutions. Fortunately, an introvert's natural penchant for thoughtful observation is well suited to seek out leaks and flaws and come up with creative and productive solutions.

Adopting a problem-solver attitude, even if it's only obviating a minor difficulty, will increase your value in the eyes of employer and colleagues. I recently worked with a young professional who experienced this firsthand. While interning at an accounting firm, he noticed that a lot of paper was being wasted during the task of transferring documents. After some additional observation and careful evaluation, he confirmed that the quantity of paper used was totally unnecessary and found an alternative sustainable method for getting the job done while eliminating waste. His company consequently adopted his suggestion and greatly appreciated the intern's ability to save the company money and time. Best of all, the employer recognized this intern's star potential and hired him for a full-time position.

The lesson here is: Tap into your nature and be aware of the actions and interactions that take place around you, either in the office or virtually. Listening and observing are your strengths and can lead to identifying problems that others in their haste have missed. The next step of suggesting

constructive solutions will make the workplace hum and can bring substantial rewards.

Saving your employer time and money will certainly win you applause,
but discovering ways to create workplace harmony can get you a standing
ovation. If you notice evidence of misunderstandings or interpersonal conflict, have the courage to point it out. Then, diplomatically suggest ways
that might enhance work relationships to make the office a more coopera-
tive place overall.

Mariana, a medical sales professional, demonstrated this scenario when
she observed a disconnect between her colleagues, partly due to their work,
which demands being on the road a great deal. Through conversations
with her colleagues, Mariana found that they felt isolated, particularly be-
moaning the lack of opportunity to touch base with one another and establish a supportive network. Stressing that this was not a personal issue
but widespread among her colleagues, Mariana described her findings to
the district manager and articulated a scenario that would further support
communication and strengthen morale. She came to her VP with clear
evidence of a situation that was universal to the sales reps and presented
a viable approach to fix it. Mariana was then given the approval to design
and deliver team-building workshops that led to a more engaged staff and
higher, team-oriented performance.

Commit to Learning

In this work era of high expectations and results, it would be a form of
suicide to simply rest on your laurels after a successful project, or expect to
get promoted by sitting smugly at your desk. Constant learning and sustained, committed effort to sharpen your skills are critical keys to accessing
that desirable corner office. So whether through formal or informal means,
make a concerted effort to keep up with the latest information and techniques; otherwise, no matter how hard you work, or what you have already
accomplished, you will become obsolete.

Although it is always satisfying to exercise your basic talents and personal passions, don't let the fact that you are not particularly interested in
computer training stop you from learning a new database that will increase

your efficiency. A training program may not seem exciting to you—it may even intimidate you—but sign up anyway. If you are an entrepreneur, you might benefit from learning cutting-edge techniques that have the potential to attract more clients or customers or offer better ways to manage the business.

Take full advantage of internal opportunities offered by your company's training department. It won't cost you a penny, but it will establish you as an eager employee and give you invaluable proficiency. You can also increase your knowledge by reading trade or professional magazines, as well as mainstream publications like the *Wall Street Journal*.

Ensuring that your choices are in line with your career goals, you may also want to take a course or earn a degree or certificate. The educational benefits will give you a firm foundation in the workplace, as well as expedite your climb to the next professional level or unlock doors that lead to a totally new career field.

Be on the lookout for opportunities that will increase your professional knowledge base, such as seminars, conferences, or webinars. Online learning in particular can be a great way to build knowledge when you have a demanding work schedule or have a busy home life. There are strong incentives for taking advantage of any means that will brighten your morale and make you more work smart. Beyond the obvious fact that these will help you stretch your cerebral muscles, they will also increase your marketability. Learning to master material that is relevant and new will add to your self-esteem and give you further reason to step forth with confidence.

Meet Leaders and Experts

Identifying and interviewing thought leaders in your field is a step in the right direction, but not necessarily the same as networking for a new opportunity. Gaining a supportive mentor is a great result, but your main goal is to gain insight and wisdom that will help you grow professionally. Don't assume that these industry leaders are too busy to talk. Put aside any hesitation that might be the result of channeling your shy, nervous, or intimidated self by realizing that these "leaders" did not suddenly and magically land in a position of authority. Often they enjoy sharing what experience and success has taught them. It is very likely that they gained these only because some other leader and expert acted as mentor to them somewhere along their own career path. Remember: You are not aiming to secure a new job; rather, you are exploring ways that a respected expert can expand and encourage your own career. Find such leaders by using LinkedIn, by way of referrals, tapping into alumni networks, or by attending an event at which a leader speaks on a panel or is scheduled to give a presentation.

Thinking outside the box can be risky, but there are times when stretching yourself yields rich rewards. My client Shoshanna, a quiet finance professional, read an article in the local business journal about a CFO of a small investment management company, whom she had followed and admired for years. The article highlighted the company's technology innovations and the fact that the company's wealth platform was ranked as the leading wealth-management solution. Also mentioned was how the CFO helped navigate a complex merger with two banks. I encouraged Shoshanna to reach out to him, so she took a chance and sent a note through LinkedIn. She mentioned the article and her admiration for his work, and asked if he might be willing to meet with her at a convenient date and time so she could learn more about his career path. Shoshanna assumed that she would never hear back, so she was pleasantly surprised when she received a favorable response. She had taken a risk in contacting him because her request might have easily been dismissed, but what did she have to lose? She had everything to gain by taking action; at worst, she'd receive a minor snubbing and move on to plan B, C, or D.

Up-front and personal meetings work very well for introverts because you are the star of one-on-one engagement; you won't need to compete for the leader's attention with a gaggle of others. In this personal type of meeting, you can show your genuine interest by delving more deeply into this industry leader's history, background, and philosophy—again, in tune with your introvert's mindset. Plus, you will be doing so on the introvert's turf, a more serene atmosphere that speaks to a deeper connection. However, don't shy away from a phone meeting if face-to-face isn't possible because of schedule or geographic location.

Questions to Ask an Expert

⇨ Who has had the most impact on your leadership style or career?

⇨ How do you encourage creative thinking and innovative ideas?

⇨ How do you keep employees motivated?

⇨ What are the most important decisions you make as a leader in your organization?

⇨ What are some of the ways in which you think leaders fail?

⇨ If you have two equally qualified candidates, how do you decide which one to hire?

⇨ What's the key to succeeding in this field or industry?

⇨ What do you do to continue growing professionally?

Networking: Part Two

In Chapter 5, we discussed ways to build and take advantage of your network. If you want to thrive in your career, take networking up another notch. Although you might be reserved and sensitive, introverts can find many creative and comfortable approaches to establish and sustain healthy professional networks throughout their working lives. Think of professional relationships as the fuel that accelerates your career and ensures that you don't find yourself with an empty tank at any crucial point in your career.

Four Ways to Supercharge Your Network

1. **Lunch:** Getting out of your company confines or home office at lunch time can clear your head and refresh your spirit, while creating an ideal opportunity to establish a more effective one-on-one working relationship with a colleague or supervisor. There will always be crunch times at work. But don't become so immersed in the fray that you don't take some time to schedule one or two lunches a month with a colleague or mentor. Your introvert comfort zone is a tempting and seductive place, so stepping out of it periodically is a move you should take seriously. Shake yourself

loose from that safe place and go out to lunch with someone who you don't know well, but who you would enjoy getting to know or prosper from knowing better. Remember: Face-to-face is the best approach in relationships, and it is often your forte.

2. **Board of advisors:** Consider organizing your own board of advisors who can help you evaluate where you stand in your career. Checking in periodically with colleagues and leaders in this forum can be a reassuring morale booster, especially if this group can give you objective tips that guide and support you professionally. Your board might include current or past bosses or mentors, and colleagues who have been promoted to higher levels because of their knowledge and experience. Professionals such as these can be a valuable sounding board when you want to mobilize your career and are searching for advice and direction toward new opportunities. Think of this mechanism as a barometer that reflects how well you perform, nudges you when you fall short, and provides an honest assessment of your potential and future goals.

3. **Keep in touch:** It's important to keep an open line with your key contacts. Consider how supportive their advice and counsel could be if you are faced with a sudden layoff or a firm decision to find a new position. Recruit at least three senior-level contacts in your network who agree to serve as references, and who you are confident will provide favorable recommendations on your behalf. They will be useful when you are a finalist for a new job or pursuing an advanced degree and need to provide names of those who know your work and can provide reasons why you are the best candidate.

4. **Give back:** While you continue to build your network, consider ways you can reciprocate. Give some equally worthy advice and council to one of your contacts when they are job hunting or at a crossroads and need guidance. Or come to their rescue by connecting them to resources that will support their goals.

For the colleague struggling with a challenging client or needing a hand tackling an organizational issue, you may be their champion if you provide a contact with the expertise to help resolve his or her problem. Even if you don't make the connection in person, you can rely on technology such as email or LinkedIn to provide the necessary information.

Freshen Up Your Resume and LinkedIn Profile

Your resume should be updated periodically and ready for action at a moment's notice. This may seem rudimentary, but I have worked with numerous clients whose resumes no longer reflected the professional person they had become. Despite notable work throughout the last three to five years, they simply neglected to bring their resume up to date to reflect how they had grown with the times. To avoid having to reconstruct these items later—and often losing essential elements in the process—keep a running list of key projects noting achievements, skills, and results attained.

Every six months to a year, refresh and renew your resume so that it offers a true picture of the accomplished professional you have become. Do the same for your LinkedIn profile. The time you dedicate now will save a mountain of work later; then, without frantically scrambling to collect bits and pieces of your history, you will be fully prepared the moment a new opportunity presents itself. Your resume will be polished, current, and impactful, and you'll be off to the races.

Let Your Voice Be Heard

The work world is an extroverted place requiring voices to sound out opinions and suggestions during meetings and company events. You may find yourself in a position that demands formal presentations of reports or lengthier public speaking engagements such as workshops or seminars. These are eminently achievable by relying on familiar aspects of your natural introversion and tapping into available extrovert skills.

Most introverts learn to face the reality that career success involves speaking and relating to others—and this can't be accomplished without standing up and being heard. The good news is that you can succeed without abandoning your introverted energies, jettisoning your style, or sinking into pessimism.

The Three Golden Rules for Speaking Up

My three rules for speaking up are simple to follow and easy to apply. Over time, they will build your confidence, which can help melt away anxiety and guide you in your approach to individual and group meetings. As a result, you will realize that you have seminal contributions to make, and that you are indeed a powerful force in the organization and life of your clients and customers.

1. **Reflect:** Time to think is a powerful element in the development of ideas and the solution to problems. It is in your nature to quietly open the door to novel inventions and to methodically tinker with issues until you find a solution.

2. **Prepare:** Organize your thoughts or questions in advance. It helps to fire up the synapses in the brain when you write things down, so outline a few pertinent ideas or generate a bulleted list that represents the points you want to convey. If it's a more formal presentation during which you will deliver a report, this rule still applies as a way of summarizing what you will say and making sure that the information your audience receives is clear. In most situations, you can have your thoughts and questions in your iPad or notebook. These are not crutches but aides to help you maintain focus and stay on point. Advance preparation feeds confidence and helps you avoid distractions from all the extroverted, head-spinning energy surrounding you.

3. **Rehearse:** This does not have to be an arduous and time-consuming task. It may be enough to simply review your notes a few times in a quiet and relaxed space. If you feel especially nervous because the meeting or event is particularly important, or you will be appearing before a large group, enlist a colleague or trusted friend for support and feedback as you practice. If you are still not completely reassured, consider using creative visualization or the meditation techniques discussed earlier to enhance a positive feeling and calm your shaky nerves.

Diplomatic Interruption

Even with advance planning, you may still feel silenced by the big egos in the meeting room who make it their mission to be seen and heard by diving into any discussion full force. But sometimes a whisper is more impactful than a shout. Learn to use what I call "diplomatic interruption" so you don't get lost in the crowd. Without any hint of offense, you might gently interject: "Excuse me, but something you just said triggered a new idea on how to approach the problem." Or you might add: "This was a good discussion, but before we move on I would like to present a quick synopsis related to the market survey."

If an idea or solution is presented that agrees with what you were going to say, you might offer support, such as, "That's a great idea. We could even add to the program by . . ." Your "interruption" will be more than welcome because you were able to validate the speaker's idea or comment while simultaneously presenting your original spin on the topic.

Public Speaking

Your job description might require that you develop and present a workshop or webinar, deliver a talk, or even a TED Talk. Almost everyone experiences a touch of performance anxiety when faced with a substantial presentation in front of an important audience. Stereotypes always include myths, and a big myth is that introverts are not good at public speaking. However, it is exactly your love of careful, methodical thought that produces unique content and an insightful, well-researched presentation. If you don't have much on-stage experience, you may need to give more attention to rule 3, "Rehearse."

Understanding Anxiety

Awareness facilitates control. Trying to ignore your nervous feelings, on the other hand, will only blow those out of proportion, and your body will react no matter how much you deny the signs. So recognize and admit what you are feeling; anxiety floods your brain with warning signals and your body with hormones that elevate your heart rate and blood pressure.

When you are anxious and full of worry, your body reacts with signals like stomach knots, shallow breathing, shaky hands, or a quivering voice. Accepting and noticing your emotional state can be the first step toward placing the negative anticipation into perspective and controlling the fear. Believe it or not, fear has a positive side, too. In supercharging your body, fear gives you an energy you can use equally to your advantage when in a public speaking forum.

Tips to Manage Public Speaking Anxiety

⇨ **Follow the three golden rules for speaking up,** but spend more quality time on rule 3: Rehearse and practice your presentation.

⇨ **Remember to speak clearly and project your voice** at a confident level during your practice sessions. Catch yourself if you speak too quickly and slow it down.

⇨ **Know your audience.** Make sure you are on the same page with the organization's contact person regarding the topic and time length of presentation.

⇨ **Think positively.** Expect to engage successfully with the audience.

⇨ **Take time for aerobic exercise** the night or morning before a presentation, which can reduce adrenaline levels and anxiety by 50 percent, according to several studies.

⇨ **Arrive early to check on equipment,** including the podium, microphone, and other audiovisuals.

⇨ **Use anxiety reduction techniques,** such as deep breathing, visualization, or movement.

⇨ **View anxiety symptoms as indicative of excitement,** not a precursor to flopping.

⇨ **Keep notes or a PowerPoint presentation handout within reach** in case you lose your train of thought during your presentation.

⇨ **Use tools that break up the occasional monotony of a verbal presentation,** such as PowerPoint slides, video clips, and handouts. Diverting the audience's attention will also reduce some of their focus on you.

⇨ **Bring water.** You may need to lubricate your voice if it gets dry.

⇨ **Look at friendly faces in the audience.** Most of the time, audiences want you to succeed and are on your side.

Don't be discouraged if you have a few bad experiences; nobody gets standing ovations every time. Assess what the problem is, and find ways to conquer it the next time around. I was once presenting a workshop on careers in law to an audience of fifty people when I became slightly dizzy and couldn't collect my thoughts. The temperature in the room was very warm, but I may have experienced a slight panic attack. I told the group that I was a little dizzy and needed to leave the room for a moment to get a drink of water. I drank a lot from the fountain just outside of the room as I talked myself into finishing the presentation. A few deep breaths later, I returned to a room of extremely supportive people, finished the presentation, and even garnered some compliments afterward. Reflecting on what had happened, I realized I had been under a lot stress; then the combination of poor ventilation in the room and speaking too fast only aggravated my physical and psychological reactions. Now I make sure I find ways to relax and decompress from other work commitments before a presentation.

Nothing beats experience. You can help desensitize your fear by taking on more public speaking engagements. If you are really struggling or want to improve your speaking skills in front of an audience, consider taking a public speaking course. Many colleges offer non-credit and inexpensive public speaking classes. Toastmasters International, a nonprofit organization, has a long history of helping professionals become confident and engaging speakers.

Visibility

As you develop confidence, extend this skill in the communications with your manager, team, or board. Keep them informed of the status on your projects and the results you have achieved. Although introverts often prefer to think through a problem on their own, don't let that habit get in the way of soliciting support and gathering advice from your boss or senior leaders. That's their job, and you will avoid conflict and misunderstanding if you keep them informed of obstacles and aware of potential problems.

Self-Marketing

Visibility also means promoting your accomplishments to ensure your boss and colleagues are aware of how you excel in your work. This information will also inform them how to better capitalize on your unique skills. Despite what you may think, your tendency to be modest isn't an asset at work. When your project produces successful results, or you have introduced a new concept or innovative idea, make sure everyone with whom you work closely knows. You don't have to make a public announcement; send out an email to select recipients, or ask your manager's opinion on the best way to promote your achievement. Similarly, when you are given credit for an accomplishment, don't downplay your efforts or results with statements like, "It wasn't that difficult," or "It really isn't that important." A simple "Thank you" will do.

Although introverts can be strong collaborators and classic team players, be sure to give yourself credit if you have made an important contribution to a group project. In your natural, understated way, you can highlight your achievement without clouding the efforts of other members.

Let your wider circle of professional contacts know about any impressive results in your work life, as well. Again, you don't have to boast in person. Use social media or email blasts to inform your network that you published an article, won an award, or achieved something unique in your work.

Survive the Future and Adapt to Change

Looking ahead to the future, it's impossible to say what tomorrow's workplace will bring—what transformations will occur from new trends, technology, or other forms of corporate culture. How you navigate your career moving forward will primarily depend on your willingness to adapt.

You can't fight off the future. The survival of your career will depend on your ability and willingness to accept the rapid pace of change in today's work world. Layoffs happen, unexpected firings occur, and organizations modify and morph. Your job description can change like a chameleon, you may shift jobs like seasonal clothing, and your organization's managers may come and go. There is still no escaping this inevitable flux whether you are an entrepreneur or working for a startup. Like sharks in continuous motion, businesses must keep moving to stay alive, quickly shifting and transitioning as they expand and grow. If you adhere to the following keys to survival, your career can outlast the speed of change.

Eight Keys to Career Survival in the Age of Acceleration

1. **Bring innovative approaches and new ideas to the workplace:**
   ⇨ What knowledge do you possess that others might not?

   ⇨ What unique or unusual insights do you have?

   ⇨ Where does your imagination take you?

2. **Identify an emerging trend that could impact your division and organization:** Read professional journals and publications, attend conferences and panel discussions, and read books that offer progressive theories and ideas.

3. **Take calculated risks:** Try something that may seem just a little intimidating. If your current work situation is causing conflict, try a new approach or adjust your strategy. Avoid getting stuck in a rut because the usual approach is seductively familiar and comfortable.

4. **Think globally to keep on top of a changing world:** Identify key trends of globalization and how it impacts market and career opportunities. Take note of the following global trends causing shifts in the workplace today:
   ⇨ The corporate world is shrinking.

   ⇨ Work is increasingly project based.

   ⇨ Competition is high.

   ⇨ Conceptual skills are more in demand.

   ⇨ Many jobs are created due to unmet needs.

5. **Be self-directed with your career:** Don't expect anyone to see the future and give you a magical vision of your career yet to come.

Along the bumpy ride of company mergers or reorganization, always be your own best advocate, and never expect that your employer will act as a benevolent uncle on your behalf. In short, take control of your career's direction.

6. **Stay savvy about your organization:** Keep abreast of what's going on throughout the organizational landscape. Listen and watch carefully to fully understand the corporate culture and behavioral norms, such as how the company is thriving, where it's faltering, and who is on their way up or out. Then, find the best way to fit yourself into the company culture without compromising who you are.

7. **Keep on top of technology:** Don't turn into an old dog that can't learn new tricks. Remain flexible, aware of current trends, and computer sharp. Technological advances continue to accelerate and are driving turbulence and change in the workplace. Unless you keep up to date and ensure that you are technically agile, you are in danger of becoming irrelevant and dispensable. Don't fear technology; embrace it as an ally, and may the force be with you as you advance your knowledge and succeed in tasks that can lead to career advancement.

8. **Be very good at what you do:** It is unrealistic to expect that you will be the headliner in every storyline at your workplace. However, your efforts, input, and results should demonstrate to management and colleagues that you are a key contributor who performs at a highly productive level. Whereas building relationships and communicating effectively both orally and in writing are important to your success story, you must equally demonstrate your ability to master major tasks and responsibilities with finesse and confidence.

Take Care of Yourself

As you know, introverts can't be "on" 100 percent of the time; you need time to restore your energy before jumping back into the stress of everyday life and work. Taking these moments to "recharge" and "unplug" from work and technology is essential to maintain a healthy work-life balance and improve your overall quality of life.

Recharge

Susan Cain, author of the bestselling book, *Quiet*, coined the term, "restorative niches," meaning "the place you go when you want to return to your true self."[2] All the energy and effort you put forth as you speak up and interact with groups in your work can easily deplete an introvert's energy. To recharge, find a moment during the day and a peaceful place to be alone, so you can return to feeling like yourself. Close your office door for a short time, take a walk during lunch or another break, or perhaps find a quiet hallway outside your office where you can decompress.

If you work at home and find yourself on the phone with clients and emailing customers all morning, take a few breaks during the day to clean your desk, go to the grocery store, or just sit in a quiet space for a while somewhere in your house or apartment. Sometimes work requires you to be "on" all day, and your restorative niche might simply be later in the day at home in front of the TV or in your bedroom reading a book.

Unplug

Employers are faced with high demands of production in this economy and expect employees to deliver strong and measurable results. Cell phones, email, and texting all conspire to accelerate work, and create clients and customers who demand immediate attention. With all these external pressures, you may work longer and harder, and could be in danger of slowly slipping into a toxic state of workaholism.

Introverts are at risk of overextending themselves, because they prefer communicating behind the scenes using technology. You may have a natural aversion to confronting challenges head-on at the time they emerge and instead find yourself using text or email after work hours to try to force the resolution of an issue. To break this habit, make a commitment to turn off your computer and cell phone before dinner or early in the evening. Otherwise, you will find yourself floating in cyberspace after hours, losing more of your time on this planet with friends and family. Face the fact that your desk will never be completely clear; that is why they call it "work." So, unless there is truly an urgent matter at hand from which you cannot divorce, give yourself an opportunity to exercise different muscles. Making time for hobbies and personal interests can rechannel your energy, and you will likely be happier and more productive in the office, too.

Work can be an energizing and powerful way to express your talents, display your skills, and make an impact. Just don't allow work to control your existence, or you will miss out on the endless array of fascinating and enlivening aspects of life that you have every right to experience and enjoy.

CONCLUSION:

FINAL THOUGHTS

My purpose for writing this book was to help you pinpoint your talents and skills and then market them to employers, so that you feel in control of your career, both now and in the future. Although I sketched out specific guidelines, recommendations, and steps, remember that career development doesn't move in a straight path. Job search and career advancement demand that you take risks, expand your skills, and learn from your mistakes while accepting the unpredictable nature of the job market and workplace. This is a road that may be fraught with fear, doubt, and cold feet, but don't take setbacks personally, as introverts tend to do. Keep in mind that this journey, bolstered with new skills and a deeper understanding of self, is one that ultimately leads to personal growth and reward.

After facing my own challenges, I have been consistently reassured by the ways in which my introverted qualities add value to my life and work. Rather than feeling inferior for shying away from occasional events or for not promoting myself as vigorously as I could, I am at peace with the quietly reflective colorations of my introversion. At the same time, I have been surprised at the benefits I've gained from efforts to lean into extroversion:

establishing new and refreshing relationships, engaging in public speaking, and taking on exciting leadership opportunities.

It might have been easier if someone had coaxed me out of my cocooning tendencies earlier in my career. But any regrets over opportunities I failed to seize were far overshadowed by the eventual discovery of my own path: the rich experience of helping clients build up their own confidence and venture out to reach their full potential.

Much has been written about the role played by resilience and the powerful impact of hope in helping people accept and adjust to the inevitable changes that life has in store for them. I would like to leave you with some deeper insight into how the two allies of resilience and hope can help you maintain optimism and continue looking ahead to a successful future in a rapidly changing world.

Resilience

It is natural to have a healthy uncertainty about the future and stay alert to the shadows that may appear around the corner. Finding ways to adjust when thrown a curveball and having the ability to bounce back are essential to managing your career. So accept failure and mistakes without tearing yourself apart. Resilience acts as the CPR that brings you back to life from any adversity.

After researching many theories, Diane Coutu, author of *How Resilience Works* and former editor of *Harvard Business Review,* identified three unique traits of resilient people:

1. Acceptance of reality
2. A sense that life is meaningful
3. An exceptional ability to improvise[1]

Even if you feel as though you don't embody all these admirable characteristics, work at them day to day. With practice, you will find that each of these can help you create a positive outlook and give you an increased sense of resilience.

How to Build Resilience

Some people seem to be born with a steady, unfailing gyroscope, landing square on their feet no matter what circumstances come at them. Even if you don't have natural balance and this enviable resilience, you don't have to feel as if you are walking on eggshells. What you may not possess naturally can be learned. The following approaches will give you the power to rebound and, particularly important, avoid a catastrophic reaction that would only make crises and setbacks even worse.

➪ **Adopt a positive outlook.** Resilience isn't a denial of loss. In fact, it is healthier to experience the emotions associated with loss, ranging from sadness and frustration to absolute anger. True resilience is the ability to absorb a punch and snap back from defeat, having accepted what occurred as a learning experience. Armed with lessons for the future, you advance toward the light at the end of the tunnel and emerge with a clear head.

A sense of humor and laughter can help you exit that tunnel quickly—and prevent feelings of despair from dragging you down along the way. After all, how many times have you looked back at a challenging life event in the rearview mirror and laughed as you realized it was not so cataclysmic as it appeared at the time?

➪ **Reach out to friends and family.** Introverts tend to keep their feelings and their personal successes and failures close to the vest, even during the most trying times. However, this kind of self-contained approach doesn't often encourage resilience. One key to bouncing back is to reach out to family and close friends and accept help from those who will listen and support you.

➪ **Assist those in need.** At the same time as accepting help, stepping out to help others in need can place your situation in perspective and increase your bounce-back factor. Adam Grant, Wharton professor and coauthor of *Option B: Facing Adversity, Building Resilience and Finding Joy,* studied a group of workers who were asked to keep a journal of their contributions. The study revealed that workers expressed receiving a significant benefit from helping others in the workplace. Grant explains,

"What really boosted resilience was focusing not on contributions received from other people but rather contributions given to other people."[2]

⇨ **Be introspective.** Resilient people have a knack for being able to ask themselves questions that stimulate and produce options. They don't harp on questions related to who is to blame or what caused their bad luck. Instead, they ask questions such as, "What's the lesson here?" and "What are my options now?" These are the kind of thoughts that often open the door to creative solutions and brilliant plans.

⇨ **Take action.** The time to set realistic goals is when you have taken a deep breath and embraced the challenge, accepted the problem, and are ready to move forward. When things are not going well, your energy may be depleted, so don't expect to improve matters in a single motion. Focus on a particular aspect of the task, and take one small step toward your goal. The sense of achievement that this creates, however tiny, will allow you to shake off some of your sluggishness and give you the necessary strength to continue along the road to success. It is a fallacy that you must be highly motivated to make something happen. Simply getting into action by making that first inroad will fuel your desire and motivation.

As an introvert, you tend to enjoy fully plumbing the depths of an issue and employing your creative thinking powers to conjure up new and interesting ideas. These qualities are always at your disposal and, not surprisingly, are in high demand in the workplace. These natural elements of your character will serve as your lifejacket in a sea of change. By combining your inherently thoughtful ways with a splash of resilience, you will improvise your way back from any unpleasant surprises or traumatic changes that may occur in your career.

Hope

The path to any successful career is marked by milestones and riddled with challenges along the way. Getting fired or laid off, or facing a job hunt that seems to have no end in sight can weigh down the most optimistic person.

You may perceive a sense of shame creeping in, along with a feeling that you have been partially robbed of your identity. This sensation of being cast aside can even result in conditional or short-term depression.

Many of my clients struggling with these types of career challenges often ask, "What's wrong with me?" It is important to look at what you have done or left undone that may have contributed to the present state of events. But while you are taking a self-inventory, remind yourself that there is no shame in losing a job or being passed over for a promotion. It has happened to many successful people.

Hope is the deep, wise voice within that assures you that you are right to see a rewarding future no matter what misadventures have come your way. It's a blend of positive thinking, enduring loss, understanding the possibilities, overcoming the hurdles, and placing you in the driver's seat.

Shane J. Lopez, PhD, was a psychologist and senior scientist at Gallup who conducted several research studies on hope. In creating his hope theory, he developed the following four main concepts:

1. The future will be better than the present.
2. I have the power to make it so.
3. There are many paths to my goals.
4. None of them is free of obstacles.[3]

Envision your career evolution as a stimulating, exciting, or even hairraising story. Embrace your introversion as a familiar friend, and challenge its nature now and again by periodic bold moves. In time these won't seem so bold at all, just another variation of your theme. Part of living your life is determined by how you ride the bumps in the road. So hold hands with hope as you walk along the path of discovery to your destiny.

Notes

Introduction

1. "A Positive Framework for Life-long People Development," Consulting Psychologist Press, *www.cpp.com/en-US/Products-and -Services/Myers-Briggs*

2. Carl Jung. *Psychological Types.* Princeton, New Jersey: Princeton University Press, 1976.

3. Robert R. McCrae. "Human Nature and Culture: A Trait Perspective," *Journal of Research in Personality* 38 (2004): 3–14.

4. Wendy Wang. "The Rise of Asian Americans," *Pew Research Center Report,* March 2012.

5. Thomas L. Friedman. *Thank You for Being Late: An Optimist's Guide to Thriving in the Age of Acceleration.* New York: Fisher, Strauss and Giroux, 2016.

6. Lawrence F. Katz and Alan B. Krueger. "The Rise and Nature of Alternative Work Arrangements in the United States, 1995– 2015," *National Bureau of Economic Research*, September 2016, Working Paper 22667.

7. Reid Hoffman and Ben Casnocha. *The Startup of You.* New York: Crown Business, 2012.

Chapter 1

1. Marti Olsen Laney. *The Introvert Advantage: How to Thrive In an Extrovert World.* New York: Workman Publishing, 2002.

Chapter 3

1. "Keeping an Eye on Recruiter Behavior," TheLadders, March 2012, *https://cdn.theladders.net/static/images/basicSite/pdfs/TheLadders-EyeTracking StudyC2.pdf*

2. Trista Winnie. "How to Create a Resume that an Applicant Tracking System Won't Ignore," April 2015, *www.jobscan.co/blog/how-to-create-a-resume-that-an-applicant-tracking-system-wont-ignore/ Jobscan*

Chapter 4

1. "About LinkedIn," *https://news.linkedin.com/about-us#statistics*

2. "Number of Monthly Active Twitter Users Worldwide from 1st Quarter 2010 to 1st Quarter 2018," Statista, *www.statista.com/statistics/282087/number-of-monthly-active-twitter-users/*

3. "Number of Monthly Active Facebook Users Worldwide as of 1st Quarter 2010 to 1st Quarter 2018," Statista, *www.statista.com/statistics/264810/number-of-monthly-active-facebook-users-worldwide/*

4. Salman Aslam. "Pinterest by the Numbers: Stats, Demographics & Fun Facts," Omnicore, January 2018, *www.omnicoreagency.com/pinterest-statistics/*

Chapter 5

1. "Survey Reveals 85% of All Jobs Are Filled via Networking," The Adler Group, 2016, *https://louadlergroup.com/new-survey-reveals-85-of-all-jobs-are-filled-via-networking/*

Chapter 6

1. "Overwhelming Majority of Companies Say Soft Skills Are Just as Important as Hard Skills," Career Builder and Harris Poll, April 10, 2014, *www.careerbuilder.com/share/aboutus/pressreleasesdetail.aspx?sd=4%2f10%2f2014&id=pr817&ed=12%2f31%2f2014*

2. "The Soft Skills Employers Want the Most," LinkedIn Survey, August 30, 2016, *https://business.linkedin.com/talent-solutions/blog/trends-and-research/2016/most-indemand-soft-skills*

3. Patty Mulder. "Communication Model by Albert Mehrabian," ToolsHero, 2012, *www.toolshero.com/communication-skills/communication-model-mehrabian/*

4. Amy Cuddy. *Presence: Bringing Your Boldest Self to Your Biggest Challenges.* New York: Little, Brown and Company, 2015.

Chapter 7

1. Michelle A. Marks and Crystal M. Harold. "Who Asks and Who Receives in Salary Negotiation," *Journal of Organizational Behavior* 32 no. 3 (March 2006).

2. Kenneth Matos and Ellen Galinsky. "2014 National Study of Employers," Society for Human Resource Management, Families and Work Institute.

Chapter 8

1. Arie Shirom, Sharon Toker, Yasmin Alkaly, Orit Jacobson, and Ran Balicer." Work-based Predictors of Mortality: A 20-Year Follow-up of Healthy Employees," *Health Psychology* 30 no. 3 (2011).

2. Mark Murphy. "Leadership IQ Study: Why New Hires Fail," *Public Management* 88 no. 2 (2006): 33.

Chapter 9

1. Gail Matthews. "Study on Setting and Writing Goals," Old Dominion University of California. January 2015.

2. Susan Cain. *Quiet: The Power of Introverts in a World that Can't Stop Talking.* New York: Crown Publishing, 2012.

Conclusion

1. Diane Coutu. "How Resilience Works," *Harvard Business Review* 80 no. 5 (2002).

2. Catherine Clifford. "Adam Grant: Resilience Is the Secret to Success," CNBC.com, June 2017, *www.cnbc.com/2017/06/06/adam-grant-how-to-improve-resilience.html*

3. Shane Lopez. *Making Hope Happen: Create the Future You Want for Yourself and Others.* New York: Atria Publishing, 2013.

INDEX

ACKNOWLEDGMENTS

The more my professional knowledge grew, the more I wanted to put my experience into a book so that I could share my excitement for my work with others. I was equally excited about sharing the writing process with a community of fellow professionals, family members and valued friends. I feel so fortunate that such a rich array of backgrounds and talents have encouraged my determination and furthered the efforts that have resulted in this book.

A special thanks to Anne Dubuisson who was instrumental in helping me form the original concept and offering ideas that have provided substance and shape. Abigail Wilentz's herculean efforts and countless hours of reviewing chapters helped me refine my writing into a more polished manuscript. My appreciation to Regina Ryan, my agent, whose knowledge and persistence took me to the end zone. To the editorial staff at Career Press, please accept my genuine and deeply felt thanks for finalizing this effort with your meaningful and elegant touch. Thank you to Chris Molnar for coaching me through my fears and energizing me to move forward.

My career has been graced and upheld by so many invaluable and supportive colleagues. Gail Glicksman, my former supervisor and mentor from the University of Pennsylvania, deserves deep gratitude for giving wind to my creative energy and for nurturing my skills. Her wisdom and insight turned my job into a truly enriching career. Thanks to all my past colleagues from the University of Pennsylvania and Bryn Mawr College with special appreciation to Pat Rose, Sharon Hardy, and Debbie Becker. When I took on my first career counseling position at the Rochester Institute of Technology, Marilyn Fain Fenster was my champion and boosted my confidence. Great appreciation and a warm embrace to Diane Freedman, my former partner, and Beth Wilson who are both consummate professionals and exemplify the very best in career counseling.

No one gets far in a career in this day and age without a vital and carefully cultivated professional network. Thanks to my colleagues at the National Career Development Association (NCDA), Middle Atlantic Career Counseling Association (MACCA), The Association of Career Professionals-Philadelphia, and to many of my LinkedIn connections.

Special thanks to the many clients I have worked with throughout my career. I have learned so much from them and continue to be inspired by their determination and courage.

I am especially grateful to my friends and great supporters Jill Sneider, Tobi Goldstein, and Debbie Fox who I have had the honor and extreme pleasure of knowing since childhood. And thanks to my expansive and wonderful community of friends and family.

And to my husband, John Michel, I owe a special note of love and gratitude for his enduring tolerance and support during the development and writing of the book.